The Book On

Escape

How to Get Out of Traps You Don't Even Know You're In

The Book On Series

Jonas Calder

Published by The Book On Publishing, 2025.

First edition. August 25, 2025.

Website: https://thebookon.ca

Substack: https://thebookonpublishing.substack.com/

The Book On Escape: How to Get Out of Traps You Don't Even Know You're In

First edition. August 25, 2025.

Copyright © 2025 The Book On Publishing

ISBN: 978-1-997795-68-1

Written by Jonas Calder

The Book On Series

Table Of Contents

Dedication

For those who still think the bars are normal.

May you feel the draft of air, find the seam in the wall, and step through it.

Jonas

Author's Note

This book was born not out of theory, but out of the bruises of living. I did not set out to write a manual on escape. I set out to survive. Every page came from the moments where cages closed and breath thinned, from the choices that cut and bled but led toward air.

If you are holding this book, you already know the sensation. You have felt the subtle weight of captivity—whether in a job, a relationship, a belief system, or the quiet interior rules you never consented to. You have felt the claustrophobia and wondered if it was just you. It isn't. The bars are everywhere, but so are the exits.

This book does not offer neat formulas. It offers a posture: the discipline of refusing captivity. It is not a celebration of rebellion for its own sake. It is an insistence on living awake, even when the cost is steep.

I wrote these words to remind myself as much as to remind you. Escape is not a single act, but a lifelong practice. May these pages sharpen your vision, steady your courage, and remind you that freedom, however fragile, is worth everything it costs.
Jonas Calder

ACT ONE

Chapter 1: The Invisible Bars

You rarely notice when the walls start closing in on you. There's no clang of iron, no screech of hinges, no dramatic lock turning with finality. The bars don't arrive in the way movies teach you to expect. They come slowly, quietly, constructed from the very decisions you convinced yourself were smart, necessary, even admirable. A promotion here, a loan there, a signature scrawled across a contract you barely read. A new title, a new obligation, a new responsibility, you call progress. You clap yourself on the back for moving forward, and you don't realize until much later that every step forward was another brick sealing you inside.

The first time that realization struck me, it wasn't cinematic. No thunderstorm, no betrayal, no grand collapse. It was an ordinary Tuesday morning. The alarm screamed, the train shrieked against the tracks, and the city swallowed us all with its usual hunger. I walked into the lobby of a glass tower, swiped my badge, nodded at a guard who didn't know my name, and rode the elevator in silence with strangers who were all pretending not to exist. By the time I sat in my cubicle—a gray square I had tried to humanize with postcards and a desperate little plant—the truth slid in without permission: this isn't freedom.

It wasn't rage that struck me. It was recognition. Nobody had chained me to that desk. Nobody was holding a gun to my head. In theory, I could stand up, walk out, and never return. But in practice? I couldn't. The rent would go unpaid. The car loan would collapse. My family would question my sanity. The job title I had wrapped around myself would dissolve, and without it, I would be nothing. The cage was not physical. It was psychological, financial, and cultural. And the door, which I had always assumed was cracked open, had already been closed.

That's the cruelty of invisible bars: you don't endure them—you decorate them. You hang diplomas on them. You tape family photos across them. You polish them with words like "responsibility" and "stability" until they gleam. You point at them with pride, as though showing them off proves you're free. But the bars don't care what names you give them. They are still bars.

Once I noticed them in myself, I started seeing them everywhere. A friend of mine signed her name to student loans at eighteen. Everyone told her it was the respectable path, the ticket to independence. The numbers on the contract were abstract, like cartoon figures she would deal with later. By twenty-eight, she was crushed under the weight. Two jobs, endless overtime, weekends disappearing into exhaustion. She laughed when she called herself free. "I'm building a future," she said, even as the interest grew faster than she could pay it down. What I saw was not a future but a set of chains—legal, invisible, impossible to break.

Another friend had been married for ten years, though the love had gone stale after the first one. He stayed, he said, for his kids, for stability, for the nobility of sacrifice. He spoke the words like they were lines he had memorized for a play he no longer believed in. When he was drunk, his eyes betrayed him. Flat, tired, resigned—the eyes of a man who had built his own prison and decided to pretend it was a fortress. His bars were obligation and pride, polished daily until they almost looked like honor.

And then there are the glowing cages that hum in every hand. The smartphone was sold to us as liberation itself: work anywhere, connect instantly, broadcast endlessly. What could be freer? Yet in practice, it is a leash. Notifications tug like a chain at your pocket. Algorithms decide what you see, what you want, and what you buy. Every swipe gives away a fraction of your attention, and attention is the currency of every choice you will ever make. You insist you could put it down whenever you want, but watch your fingers twitch when it's not within reach. Freedom was promised. Dependency was delivered.

The most disturbing part is not ignorance. It's complicity. People know, at least in flashes, that they're trapped. But to admit it out loud would mean admitting they built the walls themselves. That kind of truth is unbearable. So, denial swoops in to save them. Common statements include, "This position is only temporary," "I plan to transition after my children are older," or "The timing is not appropriate at this moment." They say the marriage is going through a "rough patch." They say the phone is "a tool." "Once" acts as a shield; "just" serves as armor. But "once" never arrives. And by the time they realize it, the door is no longer ajar—it's bolted.

History has always known this trick. Roman emperors filled coliseums with bread and spectacle. Citizens roared with pride, convinced they were participants in a grand republic. In truth, their lives were scripted by the empire down to the grain in their bowls. They mistook the roar of the crowd for liberty. By the time they realized the empire owned them, it was too late.

In the twentieth century, miners in company towns thought they had steady jobs. They rose before dawn, descended into the earth, and emerged at night with their lungs full of dust. Their wages came not in dollars but in scrip—tokens redeemable only at the company store. Every cent they earned circled back into the same hands. To the miners, it looked like labor. In reality, it was containment dressed as employment, captivity written into the ledger.

Entire towns across the industrial world built their identities on factories that promised permanence. Men and women pledged loyalty, raising children who expected to inherit the same stability. For decades, the illusion held. Then the plants closed, the jobs evaporated, and the cages were revealed for what they were. Loyalty had been one-sided. The bars had always been there, but no one dared name them until it was too late.

We congratulate ourselves on being too advanced for those illusions. We say we've evolved past exploitation, that technology has liberated us. But what is social media if not the new circus? What is a mortgage if not the new company store? What is the cubicle if not a mine shaft with fluorescent lighting? We traded overseers for algorithms, whips for metrics, steel bars for glowing screens. The form has changed, but the structure hasn't.

The myth of choice keeps the whole machine running. We're told abundance equals freedom. Two hundred cereals on the shelf. A hundred streaming shows. Infinite swipes on dating apps. But choice is not liberation. It is camouflage. The man frozen in the aisle does not feel empowered; he feels anxious, paralyzed by the fear of choosing wrong. The woman swiping through endless faces does not feel valued; she feels disposable, as though she herself is another card in the deck. The family shopping for houses doesn't feel independent; they feel suffocated by thirty-year debts. Abundance conceals captivity. It doesn't dissolve it.

The psychology is devastating in its simplicity. Fear builds the walls. Pride locks the door. Loyalty guards the key. Fear whispers that leaving will ruin you. Pride warns that walking away means admitting failure. Loyalty insists you owe it to someone—your family, your employer, your country—to endure. Together, these forces form an unbreakable triangle. And so you stay. You endure. You call it sacrifice, maturity, responsibility. You tell yourself you are noble for doing what everyone else does.

I once asked an older cousin if he regretted never leaving the office where he had spent three decades. His fork clattered onto his plate. "Not everyone can run away," he snapped. "Some of us take responsibility." His anger wasn't about me. It was about the possibility that he had spent thirty years polishing bars and calling them pillars. To question his choices was to threaten the identity he had built. To walk away would mean admitting that endurance wasn't courage—it was fear wearing a mask.

Invisible cages replicate themselves through shame and defense. People mock those who try to leave. They pressure friends to stay. They ridicule risk. They call it childish, irresponsible, and selfish. They aren't being cruel. They're protecting themselves. Because if you leave and survive, it forces them to see the bars they've been ignoring. Your escape is an indictment of their captivity.

I saw this when a friend quit her job to start a business. Instead of encouragement, she was met with anxious warnings: "What about benefits? What about stability? Isn't that too risky?" Their concern sounded protective, but it was fear talking. If she succeeded, it would reveal that their cages were not inevitable but chosen. Far easier to drag her back inside than to consider climbing out themselves.

Normalization is the trap's most effective trick. If everyone agrees the cage is necessary, the cage disappears. People decorate it, upgrade it, and compete to see who has the best bars. They laugh at those who dream of leaving, dismissing them as naïve. They call resignation courage, conformity wisdom. And all the while, the bars tighten, generation after generation repeating the same defenses.

But cracks appear. They always do. A father stares at his sleeping child, realizing he doesn't want this life for them. A woman brushing her teeth, staring at a reflection she no longer recognizes. A worker pausing in traffic, struck by the absurdity of trading decades for a pension that may never materialize. These moments vanish quickly, buried under habit. But they matter. They are sparks. And sparks can burn through steel if they're fanned long enough.

The hardest part of invisible bars is not their strength but their silence. They don't clang when they close. They hum like background noise, blending into the rhythm of daily life until you can no longer tell where habit ends and captivity begins. What people call "security" is often confinement that has been normalized. Misery feels safer when it's predictable. The cage is unbearable only when you recognize it as a cage. Until then, it is simply life.

I knew a man who worked in the same factory for forty years. Every day was a copy of the one before: the same boots, the same commute, the same time clock. He told himself he was free because nobody forced him to clock in. He said it with pride, as though consistency was proof of autonomy. At his retirement party, he raised his glass and said, "I did what I was supposed to do." Everyone applauded. Later, when the noise died down, he admitted softly, "I wanted to leave a hundred times. But what would people have thought?" The factory wasn't the real cage.

The real cage was the weight of expectations, welded into his identity.

That's what makes invisible bars so effective: they become part of who you are. Fear welds them in place. Pride polishes them. Loyalty guards them. Convenience makes them comfortable. The bars don't bruise because they don't need to. They only need to keep you still.

The digital age perfected this architecture. Captivity is now wrapped in constant stimulation. The phone buzzes, the inbox fills, the calendar chimes. Each interruption is framed as a connection, productivity, or choice. In reality, they keep you from ever sitting still long enough to wonder whether the life you're living is yours. Silence is dangerous. Silence lets you think. That's why modern cages vibrate with noise. The hum keeps you distracted, docile, and contained.

And yet, cracks form. They appear in the smallest moments—on the late-night commute, when you look at the faces around you and recognize the same emptiness in your own. In the brief recall of a long-lost dream. In the fleeting clarity when you whisper to yourself, this can't be it. Most of the time, the routine swallows those thoughts whole. But once in a while, the thought lingers. And when it lingers, the whole structure begins to tremble.

That trembling is dangerous because once you name the bars, you can't unsee them. You notice the hinges, the seams, the weak spots. You realize the cage wasn't imposed—it was assembled, choice by choice, excuse by excuse. Recognition is humiliating because it exposes complicity. But it's also liberating. If you built it, maybe you can dismantle it.

Picture the man in his living room. The furniture gleams, bought on credit. The television beams images of freedom: families laughing in bright kitchens, couples driving open roads, young professionals raising glasses in rooftop bars. His phone glows, scrolling with curated feeds that promise connection while stealing his attention. On paper, he is secure. Inside, he feels the choke of obligations he can't name. The bars aren't visible, but they are there, stitched into every habit, woven into every identity. He doesn't rattle them because there is nothing to rattle. He believes the cage is life itself.

But one night, if he is lucky, he will whisper the truth: this is a cage. The whisper will echo, and the echo will grow, until the walls themselves begin to shake. That's where escape begins. Not with keys or cutters, not with drama or rebellion, but with recognition. With naming. With the daring to believe that seeing clearly is enough to change everything.

The invisible bars are the most dangerous because they are the most ordinary. They look like houses, jobs, routines, devices, obligations. They look like love, loyalty, and maturity. But once you see them for what they are, you can never go back to pretending. You either accept the cage, or you begin to fight your way out. And that moment—the moment when you admit the walls exist—is the moment your real life finally begins.

We tell ourselves cages are for other people. They are for prisoners, for captives, for the unlucky and the weak. But most of the cages people live in don't look like punishment. They look like normal life. That is why they are so difficult to escape. You don't plan a jailbreak when you don't believe you're behind bars.

I think about a neighbor I once had, a man who spent his weekends polishing a car he rarely drove. He would crouch in the driveway, rag in hand, rubbing the same fender until it gleamed like a mirror. He didn't seem to love the driving, or the mechanics, or even the car itself. He loved what it represented: proof that he had made it, that he was no longer the poor boy who had grown up on the wrong side of town. The car was his cage disguised as success. The payments kept him working long hours at a job he hated, but selling it would feel like surrender. He was bound not by the machine but by the story it told about him.

Stories are some of the strongest bars of all. They dictate what we think life is supposed to look like. The story says: go to school, get a job, buy a house, raise a family, retire. If you step off that track, you invite suspicion. People wonder what's wrong with you. Why didn't you finish college? Why don't you want kids? Why did you quit your stable job? The story is a map, but it doubles as a prison. Following it keeps you predictable. Straying from it exposes you. And predictability is the lifeblood of every system that profits from human compliance.

There's an entire economy built on these invisible bars. Think of the way consumer culture works. Every advertisement promises liberation. The truck ad shows you endless open roads. The perfume ad shows you desire without consequence. The vacation package shows you blue water and white sand, a world away from your cubicle. But none of these things is freedom. They are products tied to costs that keep you working longer, paying more, tethering yourself ever tighter to the system that sells them. The more desperately you chase the image of freedom, the deeper you bury yourself in captivity.

This is not an accident. A free population is dangerous. People who can walk away cannot be controlled. People who don't need what you're selling won't buy it. That is why the myth of freedom is maintained so aggressively. You must be convinced that freedom is already yours, that it lives in your possessions, your job, your status. If you begin to suspect otherwise, the entire structure trembles.

But for all its power, the illusion isn't unbreakable. History is filled with people who saw the bars and decided to leave, no matter the cost. Some fled oppressive regimes, walking across deserts or stowing away on ships with nothing but the clothes on their backs. Others broke from cultural cages—women who refused marriages, workers who organized strikes, artists who abandoned respectable careers to paint, write, or perform. Their decisions were mocked, punished, and resisted. Many failed. But some didn't. And those few proved the cage was never absolute.

The danger of invisible bars is that they shrink your imagination. They make the cage seem like the entire world. Escaping begins with expanding your vision beyond the walls. That expansion often comes in moments of quiet revolt. A mother deciding to take night classes after her children are asleep, refusing to let her identity end with caretaking. A young man quitting a job that is killing him slowly, even if it means couch-surfing for months. These are not tidy victories. They are messy, frightening, and uncertain. But they are the cracks where light gets in.

The man in his living room, staring at the glow of his television, may not realize that he has already begun his escape the moment he whispers, This is a cage. That whisper is rebellion. That whisper is a possibility. From there, the question is no longer whether the bars exist—they do—but whether he dares to test their strength.

Invisible bars are the most ordinary, the most invisible, and the most deadly to the human spirit. They suffocate not with violence but with comfort, with routine, with the dull reassurance that this is simply what life is. To see them is painful. To admit them is shameful. To name them is dangerous. But only when you do those things does escape become possible. And once you have seen them, the rest of your life becomes a decision: keep decorating the cage, or find a way out.

Chapter 2: The Myth of Freedom

Freedom is a word that sells better than anything else. It is pasted across billboards, sung in anthems, carved into stone, and whispered like a prayer. Entire nations build their identity around it. Corporations borrow it to market their products, slipping it into taglines so casually you barely notice. It's the one word you are not supposed to question. Who could be against freedom? To doubt it is to doubt something almost sacred. That unquestioned reverence is what gives the myth its power.

When I was younger, I believed freedom meant options. The more choices you have, the freer you must be. If I could walk into a supermarket and pick between two hundred brands of cereal, then surely I was living at the peak of liberty. If I could scroll through endless shows, playlists, or dating profiles, then I was overflowing with independence. At least that's what I told myself. But the more choices I collected, the less liberated I felt. Too many options became a kind of paralysis, a cloud of anxiety disguised as autonomy. I wasn't free. I was overwhelmed.

This is the first trick of the myth: it confuses choice with freedom. A man staring at a wall of cereals doesn't feel empowered—he feels lost, afraid of choosing wrong. A voter staring at a ballot with a dozen names feels powerful for a moment, but the illusion fades quickly. The choices all orbit the same center, bound by the same interests, designed to keep the structure intact no matter who wins. It looks like freedom, but it is only permission to pick between cages. Abundance of choice becomes camouflage for control. As long as you're distracted by the illusion of options, you don't ask harder questions about who built the aisle, who programmed the algorithm, and who benefits from keeping you spinning in circles.

The myth thrives because it doesn't mask captivity; it sells it back to you as progress. Ask the man drowning in student loans if he feels free. Ask the gig worker, refreshing his phone at midnight, waiting for the next ride or delivery to appear, told he is his own boss while an algorithm dictates his worth minute by minute. He wears the word 'freedom' like a badge, but he is bound tighter than any office employee. Ask the gig worker, refreshing his app to catch the next ride or delivery, proudly calling himself his own boss, while an algorithm decides his worth minute by minute. They all wear the word freedom like a badge. In truth, they are shackled by contracts, debts, and systems that never needed to raise a whip because the bars are built into the structure of everyday life.

Debt is the clearest example. At eighteen, you sign a loan agreement with numbers so big they might as well be imaginary. Everyone assures you it's wise, respectable, the necessary path to independence. They call it an investment. You don't understand the weight until a decade later, when you're working weekends to pay the interest. Suddenly, the freedom you were promised has curdled into servitude. You can't walk away. You can't breathe without calculating what you owe. The word adulthood is used to sanitize the cage, but the reality is closer to indenture.

Marriage can become another version of this. I knew a man who stayed in a marriage long after the love had died. He called it loyalty. He called it a sacrifice. He repeated the words until they sounded noble, but his eyes betrayed him. They were flat, dulled by years of quiet misery. He had chosen his own captivity, and because the myth told him sacrifice was freedom, he wore his shackles like medals. He convinced himself that endurance was liberty, even as it drained his life of vitality.

And then there are the glowing rectangles in our pockets. When smartphones first appeared, they were marketed as liberation itself—work anywhere, connect instantly, access infinite information. What could be freer? Yet in practice, the phone is a leash. Notifications tug at you, algorithms shape your desires, and companies profit off every tap and swipe. The leash is invisible, and that makes it stronger than iron. You insist you can put it down whenever you want, but your body betrays you. The itch in your fingers, the anxiety when the screen is dark— these are not signs of freedom. They are proof of dependency.

History has never lacked for myths of freedom. Roman emperors distributed bread and held violent spectacles to persuade citizens they were part of a grand republic. In reality, their lives were controlled down to the grain in their bowls. Indentured servants in colonial America signed contracts promising eventual release. They told themselves they weren't slaves, workers serving time. For seven years, they were bound body and soul to their masters, kept compliant by the illusion of eventual freedom.

The modern versions are slicker but no less binding. Jobs are framed as independent because you earn your own living. But quit, and the chains reveal themselves—no income, no insurance, no safety net. Mortgages are sold as ownership because you're a homeowner now. But stop paying, and the house vanishes, along with your credit and reputation. Voting is called freedom because it gives you a voice. But between elections, the system runs without you, indifferent to your existence. The choices exist, but every option is shaped by penalties. That's not freedom. That's managed obedience.

I once had a colleague who bragged about being able to walk away from his job at any time. "I'm not chained to this place," he said. "If I get tired of it, I'll quit." His words sounded bold, but his life told another story. His mortgage was tied to his salary. His children's tuition depended on his bonuses. His wife's sense of stability hinged on their lifestyle. In theory, he could leave. In practice, the cost would be ruin. His freedom existed only in bedtime stories he told himself to survive the days.

That's the genius of the myth. It convinces you that captivity is voluntary. You stay not because you must, but because you want to. You call it loyalty, responsibility, and maturity. You repeat the words until they become incantations. The door is technically unlocked, but every exit carries devastation. The myth whispers that staying is noble, that chains are commitments, that cages are homes. And you nod along, grateful for the bars that promise safety while stealing your life in increments.

Language is the myth's most powerful weapon. We don't say enslaved by debt; we say "investing in the future." We don't say trapped in a loveless marriage; we say "committed." We don't say addicted to a device; we say "connected." Words are buffers, smoothing the jagged edges of reality until we can live with them. Repeat them often enough and they harden into common sense.

"That's life," people shrug. "That's what adults do." But scratch the surface and you see what those phrases mean: don't question the cage.

The louder the word freedom is shouted, the less it usually applies. That is why it is plastered across billboards, sung in stadiums, and rolled out in every political season. If freedom were real, it wouldn't need advertising. Nobody chants "oxygen" at a rally because oxygen doesn't need defending. It's simply there. Freedom that must be constantly marketed is freedom that doesn't exist.

The paradox is brutal: real freedom is not comfortable. It is not security, not stability, not guaranteed happiness. Real freedom is risk. It is stepping into uncertainty without a net. That is why so few pursue it. The myth is easier. The myth promises you already have what you need. You are told that your choices—the job, the mortgage, the marriage, the screen—are freedom itself. You are not to ask whether these choices are binding you more tightly each day.

I remember once standing in a city on Independence Day. Flags hung from porches, fireworks popped against the sky, and children waved sparklers in the dark. People cheered and laughed, their voices carrying the pride of a nation built on liberty. But if you looked past the celebration, you saw bartenders working double shifts, nurses hurrying into night rotations, and delivery drivers weaving through traffic. They weren't celebrating freedom. They were grinding, keeping the machine running so everyone else could party. Their lives were not their own, yet the word freedom boomed from every loudspeaker. The louder the claim, the greater the denial underneath.

The myth doesn't soothe individuals. It sustains entire systems. Economies depend on people believing they are free even when they are bound. A worker convinced he has chosen his job is less likely to revolt. A citizen convinced that voting equals autonomy is easier to govern. A consumer convinced that buying equals liberty will work harder to spend more. Every illusion of freedom reinforces obedience. The cage is efficient because it makes you believe you built it yourself.

I once asked a group of students what freedom meant to them. One said, "Being able to do whatever I want." Another said, "Making my own decisions." But when I pressed them, the answers grew hollow. Could they leave their university without drowning in debt? Could they ignore the pressure to pick "safe" careers that their parents approved of? Could they refuse the constant push to curate perfect lives online? Each question revealed that their "freedom" had already been defined for them. They were free to choose between cages, but not free to walk away from the system of cages itself.

This is the quiet cruelty: captivity that feels voluntary is the hardest to escape. If you believe you are free, you will never look for the door. You'll defend your chains, polish them, boast about them. You'll shame others for even wanting to leave. You'll tell yourself stories about loyalty, duty, maturity, progress. And those stories will keep you still, year after year, decade after decade.

Yet cracks always appear. Sometimes they come in silence, in those fleeting moments when the script falters. A woman sits at her desk and suddenly wonders how many years she has left before retirement—and whether she wants to spend them all in that chair. A man paying bills pauses and wonders how much of his life has been spent keeping the lights on. These thoughts vanish quickly, drowned by routine, but they're dangerous. They are sparks. And sparks threaten the whole illusion.

When enough sparks catch, the myth falters. You see it in waves of people quitting jobs all at once, refusing to accept the endless grind as maturity. You see it in communities experimenting with different ways of living, rejecting mortgages and 9-to-5s for something less predictable but more alive. These movements are messy, disorganized, and often mocked. But they matter because they expose the lie: if freedom is real, it cannot be standardized. It cannot be mass-produced. It must be chosen in defiance of the structures designed to contain it.

The myth of freedom is powerful because it doesn't whisper to individuals—it seeps into entire cultures until it feels like the air everyone breathes. When something is everywhere, it becomes invisible. No one questions water when they're swimming in it. In the same way, people rarely stop to ask whether what they call freedom is anything more than habit, marketing, and ritual.

Think about national holidays. Independence Days, Bastille Days, Liberation Days. They are all celebrated with fireworks, parades, and speeches. Leaders stand before crowds and declare that their people are free, as though saying it often enough makes it true. But the very citizens waving flags and cheering often go home to bills that strangle them, jobs that hollow them out, and screens that mediate every waking thought. They don't feel free, but to admit that would be treasonous—not to the state, but to the story that binds them to the state.

I once watched a parade from the sidelines. Soldiers marched, bands played, and families waved little flags. The mood was infectious, and for a few minutes I felt it too—that swelling pride, that sense of belonging to something vast. But then I noticed a woman in uniform standing off to the side, holding a child in her arms. Her face was blank, tired, as if she had been emptied of everything but duty. For her, the word freedom meant long deployments, missed birthdays, and debts waiting at home. She clapped when the crowd clapped, but there was no conviction in her eyes. She understood something that the cheering crowd preferred not to see: slogans don't erase captivity.

Corporations are masters at this sleight of hand. They sell freedom as a product you can buy. A truck commercial shows a man barreling down an empty desert road, dust rising behind him, a wide horizon ahead. The message is clear: buy this vehicle and you will be unchained. A phone ad shows friends laughing together in a sunlit city, their devices glowing in their hands. Buy the phone, the ad says, and you will be connected, empowered, free. But each product comes with payments, contracts, and upgrades that lock you in. You don't buy freedom. You buy installments of captivity dressed as a lifestyle.

It isn't only material. Cultural myths of freedom shape the paths people take without realizing it. A student chooses a "safe" career not because they want it but because the fear of failure cages them before they even begin. A young couple buys a house not because they crave ownership but because renting feels like failure in a culture that equates mortgages with maturity. A worker takes on overtime not because they need to, but because hustle is branded as liberty—the freedom to "make something of yourself." At every turn, the myth converts insecurity into obedience.

The tragedy is that many defend this obedience as though it were sacred. Point out the bars, and you'll be accused of being ungrateful. "You don't realize how lucky you are," they'll say. "People in other countries don't have these opportunities." Gratitude is weaponized to silence doubt. But comparison doesn't create freedom. It only creates resignation. Saying "someone else has it worse" doesn't erase your own captivity—it makes you ashamed of noticing it.

I once met a man who called himself free because he could travel anywhere. He had a passport full of stamps, photos from cities around the world. But when I asked him if he could stop working tomorrow, his smile faltered. "Well, not yet," he admitted. His trips were paid for with credit. His adventures were financed by a job that consumed his hours and his health. He wasn't free. He was on temporary furlough from his cage, renting small tastes of liberty before returning to the grind. He defended his choices fiercely, but underneath was the truth: mobility isn't freedom when you are tethered by debt.

Even the idea of independence itself has been bent into a trap. The myth says: stand on your own two feet, rely on nobody, carve your own path. It sounds bold. But what it often creates is isolation, loneliness, and burnout. A culture that worships independence produces people too ashamed to ask for help, too afraid to admit they need others. They chain themselves to exhaustion, all while insisting they are free because they did it alone.

The irony is that real freedom usually requires interdependence. Nobody escapes alone. Even fugitives need safe houses, allies, someone to watch their back. But the myth insists you must do everything solo, because isolation makes people easier to control. A lonely person is easier to sell to, easier to manipulate, easier to keep in line.

Everywhere you look, the word freedom is wrapped around systems that thrive on keeping people compliant. It's a label pasted on cages, a ribbon tied to shackles, a chorus shouted loud enough to drown out doubt. And because everyone repeats it, you begin to believe it. You tell yourself you are free because you chose your job, your partner, your home, your devices. But the menu you ordered from was written by someone else. The boundaries of your choices were drawn long before you arrived.

The scariest part is how willingly people participate. They hang flags on their porches, wear logos on their shirts, line up for the newest device—all while insisting these rituals prove they are independent. They don't see that the rituals themselves are the bars. The pride they feel is real, but it's pride inside a cage. And pride is one of the strongest locks, because once you've staked your identity on the cage, leaving feels like death.

The myth of freedom survives because it is comfortable. It gives people the illusion of dignity without the cost of risk. If you believe you are already free, you don't have to uproot your life.

You don't have to face the terror of uncertainty. You can stay in the job you dislike, the marriage that drains you, the routines that suffocate you, all while telling yourself you are choosing them. The word freedom becomes a shield against the gnawing suspicion that you are wasting your life.

But now and then, the shield cracks. A worker who thought he was secure gets laid off without warning, and suddenly his "freedom" reveals itself as dependence. A family that thought they owned their home misses a few payments and watches the bank reclaim it. A generation raised on the internet begins to see that their every preference, every search, every movement is tracked, stored, and sold. They realize their so-called freedom of choice has been engineered, nudged, and monetized. And when the myth collapses, the grief is heavy.

I once spoke to a woman who had chased the dream of freedom her whole life. She had worked her way through college, bought a house, raised children, and built a career. She had done everything the story told her to do. When her children left home and her mortgage was finally paid, she expected to feel liberated. Instead, she felt hollow. "I thought freedom was what waited at the end," she said quietly. "But now I realize I don't know what freedom even is." She wasn't angry. She was tired, as though she had run a marathon only to discover the finish line was painted on a wall.

That is the cruelty of the myth. It doesn't only waste years— it drains meaning. People spend their lives chasing an idea that dissolves when they touch it. And because the myth is shared by millions, they rarely admit it. They smile in photos, boast on social media, and defend their choices at dinner parties. To do otherwise would be to confess that the cage they've spent decades polishing was never freedom at all.

And yet, recognizing the myth is not despair. It is the beginning of clarity. The moment you stop equating choice with liberty, comfort with independence, or ownership with autonomy, the ground begins to shift. You see how debt, devices, contracts, and cultural stories have disguised captivity as progress. You see that what was sold to you as maturity may in fact be surrender. And once you see that, you cannot unsee it.

The recognition hurts. It strips away the slogans, the pride, the illusions that kept you numb. But it also gives you something rare: the chance to want more. Real freedom, the kind that terrifies as much as it excites, begins with refusing to accept the myth. It begins with admitting that what you have been calling liberty is another set of invisible bars.

The man in the cereal aisle, the woman swiping through faces, the worker refreshing his app, the retiree staring at an empty horizon—they are all trapped in the same story. Some will stay there, because staying is easier. But some will feel the weight of the lie and decide they would rather risk the unknown than rot inside a cage decorated with slogans.

The myth of freedom is powerful. But more powerful still. To name the myth is to weaken it. To see the bars is to imagine breaking them. And to imagine is the first act of rebellion.

Chapter 3: Trap Psychology

If the bars of a cage are built from obligations, contracts, and routines, then the locks that keep them shut are hidden inside the mind. A cage without a lock is only an inconvenience. You can rattle it, test the hinges, maybe even slip out. But when the mind collaborates with the cage, when it insists that leaving is impossible or wrong, then the trap is complete. This is the cruel genius of captivity: you don't need guards when the prisoner polices themselves.

Fear is the first and most obvious lock. It doesn't always appear as terror. Sometimes it's unease, a whisper at the back of your mind that says: don't. Don't quit, don't leave, don't speak, don't change. Fear is subtle, practical, dressed in the language of caution. It tells you that the rent won't get paid, that your reputation will be ruined, and that you'll end up alone. It pretends to protect you, but what it does is immobilize you. Fear convinces you the cage is safer than the open air.

I once knew a man who had a chance to start his own business. He had ideas, contacts, and the skill to make it work. But every time he thought about leaving his job, his stomach knotted. He saw images of bankruptcy, of his family turning against him, of himself sitting in a dark apartment with the lights cut off. None of these things had happened, but fear painted them vividly enough that they might as well have. He stayed in the job, year after year, not because the bars were unbreakable but because fear whispered that the open door led to ruin.

Closely tied to fear is inertia. Inertia is not as dramatic, but it is as deadly. It's the heaviness that sets in after years of routine. Once you've lived the same way long enough, changing direction feels unnatural, even when you know you should. The mind becomes addicted to patterns. Wake at this hour, commute this road, sit at this desk, collect this paycheck. The pattern is mindless, but it is familiar, and familiarity can feel like safety.

I saw this in a colleague who had been miserable in his job for decades. He had offers elsewhere, he had valuable skills, but when I asked why he didn't leave, he shrugged. "I wouldn't even know what else to do," he said. His resignation wasn't about external limits. It was inertia. He had been in his cage for so long that the idea of walking out felt like leaping into space without gravity to guide him. The cage may have been miserable, but at least it was solid.

Then there is pride, the lock that polishes the bars until they gleam. Pride insists that you cannot leave because leaving would admit defeat. If you walk away from the job, it means you wasted the years you spent climbing. If you end the relationship, it means you chose wrong in the first place. Pride whispers that endurance is nobility, that staying proves your strength. In truth, pride is the ego's way of keeping you trapped. It is better to suffer and appear steadfast than to admit you built the wrong life.

A friend of mine stayed in a marriage long past its expiration date. He admitted he was unhappy, even miserable, but he insisted he couldn't leave. When pressed, he didn't talk about money or logistics. He talked about appearances. "What would people think?" he asked. "What would it say about me if I gave up?" Pride told him it was better to rot in silence than to risk humiliation. The cage didn't even need to close around him. Pride did the work for it.

And then there is loyalty, perhaps the most complicated lock of all. Loyalty can be beautiful in its pure form—commitment to family, community, cause. But loyalty, twisted by culture and expectation, becomes a trap. It convinces you that leaving is betrayal, that freedom is selfishness. You owe your employer, your partner, your country. You are told that abandoning the cage would be abandoning the people who depend on you. Loyalty transforms captivity into morality.

I once met a nurse who worked in a hospital that drained her to the bone. She complained endlessly about the hours, the pay, and the lack of respect. But when asked why she didn't find work elsewhere, her answer was instant: "Because they need me." She wasn't wrong—the hospital did need her. But what she didn't see was that the need was being exploited. Her sense of loyalty chained her more effectively than any contract could. She was too noble to escape. The cage had convinced her that staying was a virtue.

These four—fear, inertia, pride, loyalty—form the mental architecture of captivity. They're not separate; they overlap, reinforce, and echo each other. Fear makes you hesitate. Inertia convinces you to keep waiting. Pride makes waiting feel noble. Loyalty makes waiting feel moral. Together, they lock the door from the inside, and you hold the key but refuse to use it.

What makes these psychological traps so devastating is their invisibility. External cages at least announce themselves. You know when someone else is holding the keys. But when the trap is in your mind, you defend it. You argue for it. You make excuses for why it's necessary. You become the jailer of your own life.

The mind is clever at disguising these locks. It reframes fear as responsibility, inertia as patience, pride as resilience, and loyalty as love. Each quality sounds admirable when described in isolation. Who would criticize responsibility, patience, resilience, or love? Yet when they are used to justify a life unlived, they stop being virtues and become bars. The tragedy is that many never notice the shift. They believe they are embodying the best of human qualities when in reality they are fortifying their own prisons.

I once had a conversation with a man who prided himself on being dependable. He was the kind of colleague who never missed a deadline, who could be counted on to show up even when sick or exhausted. His boss praised him as the backbone of the company. But when I asked if he was happy, his face sagged. He admitted he wasn't. He had once dreamed of traveling, of opening his own small shop, of doing work that didn't grind him down. But responsibility had become his identity, and to let go of it felt like erasing himself. He stayed dependable. He stayed trapped.

Inertia often hides beneath the word stability. Parents will tell their children that stability is the highest goal, that a steady job, a fixed routine, and a predictable future are the marks of success. And yet stability is a slippery word. It can mean security, but it can also mean stagnation. Many confuse the two, convincing themselves they are stable when in truth they are stagnant. The difference is subtle but crucial. Stability provides a platform for growth. Stagnation is a refusal to grow at all. When inertia disguises itself as stability, you can spend decades sitting still and call it wisdom.

Pride has its own mask: perseverance. Society loves a story of perseverance, the person who endures suffering without complaint, who grinds through adversity with clenched teeth. But perseverance can also be a refusal to change course. A person can persevere in misery as easily as they can in pursuit of greatness. I once knew a woman who stayed in a toxic workplace because she wanted to prove she was tough enough to handle it. She wore her suffering as a badge of honor, as if outlasting abuse were a measure of strength. Pride convinced her that leaving would mean weakness, that escape was cowardice. But strength without direction is endurance, and endurance in the wrong place is captivity.

Loyalty, too, carries a noble face. To be loyal is to be trustworthy, to stand by others when things are difficult. But loyalty without limits becomes servitude. I've seen people stay in destructive friendships because they didn't want to "abandon" someone. I've seen workers refuse better opportunities because they felt indebted to a boss who had once given them a chance. Gratitude became an obligation, and obligation became a life sentence. Loyalty told them that leaving would make them traitors, when in fact leaving was the only way to stay whole.

The danger of these disguised locks is that they are reinforced by culture. Fear is praised as caution. Inertia is praised as consistency. Pride is praised as perseverance. Loyalty is praised as devotion. These qualities win applause, promotions, and respect. Society rewards the very traits that keep people trapped. The person who breaks free is often ridiculed as reckless or selfish. Escape is framed as failure, while captivity is framed as maturity. And because nobody wants to be seen as reckless or selfish, most people choose to stay put, polishing their bars until they shine.

I often think about how the brain resists uncertainty. Our minds are prediction machines, wired to find patterns and cling to them. When faced with the unknown, the brain lights up with warning signals. This is why change feels like danger, even when the current situation is unbearable. The body prefers familiar suffering to unfamiliar possibility. It is easier to endure a known pain than to risk a new one. This is not laziness. It is biology. But when biology goes unexamined, it becomes destiny.

Some people try to bargain with their cages. They tell themselves they'll leave once they've saved enough money, once their children are grown, once their parents no longer need them, once the timing is right. These conditions are never met because the mind simply invents new ones. The bargain is endless. The door is always a little further down the hallway. And by the time you reach it, another door has appeared. The person spends their life negotiating with locks that were never intended to open.

What makes trap psychology so devastating is how rational it sounds. Every excuse has a logic to it. Fear points to risks. Inertia points to patterns. Pride points to reputation. Loyalty points to love. Each reason is persuasive. Put them together, and they form a worldview that feels unassailable. It is only when you step back and notice how much of your life has been spent inside those rationalizations that you begin to see the truth. You weren't being reasonable. You were being restrained.

The most haunting thing about these mental locks is how quickly they become invisible. At first, you feel the tension: the fear that gnaws at you, the inertia that drags at your feet, the pride that stiffens your spine, the loyalty that tugs at your conscience. But live with them long enough, and they fade into the background. They don't vanish—they blend into the scenery until you can no longer tell where your own thoughts end and the trap begins. The cage becomes your voice. You call it your personality.

I met a man once who insisted he was cautious by nature. He claimed he had never been a risk-taker, that playing it safe was simply who he was. But as he told his story, it became clear that he hadn't always been that way. As a teenager, he had been bold, restless, curious. He had wanted to travel, to create, to push against limits. Somewhere along the way, fear had tightened its grip and inertia had set in. His identity as a "cautious man" was not natural—it was learned captivity. His psychology had reshaped itself to match the bars around him.

This reshaping happens everywhere. People say, "I'm not good with money," when they are drowning in a financial system designed to entrap them. They say, "I'm not creative," when in truth they abandoned creativity because it didn't fit the story of stability they were told to follow. They say, "I'm a loyal friend," when what they mean is that they don't know how to walk away from relationships that deplete them. The trap doesn't hold you still. It rewrites your story until the trap feels like you.

Sometimes the rewriting is so complete that people defend their cages passionately. Challenge someone's job, marriage, or way of living, and you often trigger not curiosity but rage. They lash out because to question the cage is to question them. Their pride and loyalty are so entangled with the structure of their lives that to doubt the bars would be to doubt their very existence. The more painful the truth, the harder they cling to the illusion. It is not logic that keeps them chained. It is the terror of unraveling.

Culture reinforces this entanglement. The slogans we hear— "hard work pays off," "stand by your man," "tough it out," "family above all"—sound wholesome. But beneath them lies the machinery of compliance. Hard work pays off—for someone else. Standing by your man may mean sacrificing yourself. Toughing it out might mean eroding your health. Family above all can turn into silence about abuse or neglect. The slogans serve as psychic glue, holding people in cages they might otherwise have questioned.

I often think about how children learn these lessons. A child who sees their parents miserable in work but continuing anyway absorbs that endurance as virtue. A child who watches their mother sacrifice everything for loyalty learns that love means self-erasure. A child who watches their father grind himself down out of pride learns that strength means never admitting defeat. By the time these children grow up, the locks are already installed. They don't need to be convinced to stay in cages. They already believe it is what decent people do.

The cruelty of trap psychology is that it weaponizes qualities that could be beautiful. Fear could be a caution that saves you from real danger. Inertia could be the steadiness that sustains you through storms. Pride could be confidence in real achievements. Loyalty could be love that binds people together. Instead, these qualities are twisted until they bind you to the wrong places, the wrong people, the wrong lives. They turn virtues into vices and vices into obligations.

Every so often, someone gets a glimpse of the distortion. It usually happens in quiet moments—on a long drive, in the middle of the night, at the edge of exhaustion. They feel the contradiction between the life they are living and the life they imagined. For a brief second, the bars come into focus. The fear that felt protective suddenly looks cowardly. The inertia that felt stable suddenly looks like stagnation. The pride that felt noble suddenly looks like denial. The loyalty that felt loving suddenly looks like servitude. The shock of recognition can be terrifying. Many push it away, double down on the story, and convince themselves it was a passing doubt. But some hold onto the glimpse, and in doing so, they begin the slow process of dismantling the locks.

The deepest cruelty of trap psychology is how it teaches you to doubt your own instincts. Every time a spark of rebellion flickers, the mind rushes to smother it. You think of leaving your job, and fear supplies a vivid picture of destitution. You imagine ending a relationship, and pride whispers that you will be a failure. You consider moving to another city, and loyalty reminds you of everyone who would call you selfish. The very part of you that longs for freedom is drowned by the parts that have been trained to keep you still. It is not outside authority that silences you—it is your own voice.

I once spoke with a woman who confessed she had wanted to leave her hometown for years. She had dreamed of seeing the world, of reinventing herself somewhere new. But every time she imagined buying a ticket, the arguments arrived: What if you fail? What will your parents think? Who will take care of your friends? The doubts sounded so rational that she believed them. A decade passed. Then another. One day, she realized that the window had closed—that she had aged into the very life she had once promised herself she would escape. The tragedy wasn't that she lacked opportunities. It was that her own mind had vetoed them.

This is how traps become legacies. People who never break free pass down their captivity in the form of advice. They tell their children to be careful, to be patient, to be loyal, to be strong. They mean well. They believe they are protecting them. In truth, they are handing down the same locks that held them. And so the cycle continues: fear disguised as caution, inertia disguised as stability, pride disguised as strength, loyalty disguised as love. Whole generations carry the weight, never realizing they are polishing the same bars that their parents once did.

But the cycle is not unbreakable. The first step is naming the locks for what they are. To admit that fear is not caution but paralysis. To admit that inertia is not patience but stagnation. To admit that pride is not strength but denial. To admit that loyalty is not love but servitude. Naming is dangerous because it strips away the disguises. Once you call the bars by their true names, the excuses crumble. You can no longer pretend that you are staying put for noble reasons. You are staying put because you are afraid. And when you finally say it out loud, the lock begins to weaken.

Awareness alone doesn't fling the door open. But it creates space. It allows you to imagine a different life, and imagination is the first act of rebellion. The cage relies on you not thinking about alternatives. The moment you do, the bars lose some of their power. Even if you don't act right away, even if you remain in the same place, the illusion that the cage is necessary begins to crack. You see the patterns for what they are. You see the traps not as destiny but as design. And what is designed can be dismantled.

The hardest part of escape is not breaking the bars—it is breaking the psychology that keeps you attached to them. Once you do, the bars are revealed as thinner than you imagined. The fear that once seemed overwhelming reduces to background noise. The inertia that once seemed like solidity begins to feel like suffocation. The pride that once seemed noble becomes a burden. The loyalty that once seemed beautiful reveals itself as exploitation. When these illusions collapse, the cage loses its gravity. What once felt impossible begins to look inevitable.

I think of all the people who have confessed, late in life, that they regret not leaving sooner. Their words are tinged not with sadness but with astonishment. They look back and realize the bars were never as strong as they thought. They realize they could have left years earlier if only they had questioned the voice in their head that told them to stay. Their regret is not about the cage itself. It is about mistaking the locks for truth.

Trap psychology is powerful because it is intimate. It doesn't shout at you from outside. It whispers from within. But once you recognize the voice, you can begin to answer back. You can tell fear that it is exaggerating, inertia that it is lying, pride that it is fragile, and loyalty that it has been abused. You can reclaim the qualities themselves, stripping them of their disguises and using them as tools rather than chains. Fear can sharpen your judgment without paralyzing you. Inertia can ground you without freezing you. Pride can fuel excellence without denying mistakes. Loyalty can build bonds without demanding self-erasure. The same mind that locked the door can learn to open it.

Freedom begins not with an open gate but with a shift inside the head. The cage is as much psychological as it is structural. To see that truth is unsettling, because it forces you to admit that you are complicit. But it is also liberating, because it means the key was never outside your reach. You were holding it all along.

Chapter 4: When the Door Is Already Closed

There is a peculiar silence that comes when a person realizes the door has already closed. It is not the sharp clang of a lock snapping shut, nor the rage of someone who still believes they can fight their way out. It is a quieter, heavier sound — the weight of resignation settling over a life. By the time most people recognize the cage, they are already deep inside, and the exits have grown too costly or too distant to reach. Freedom is still technically possible, but in practice it has vanished.

I remember visiting an old neighbor in a nursing home. He had worked his entire life in a job he admitted he never liked, saving for a retirement that he believed would finally set him free. For forty years, he woke before dawn, sat in traffic, endured bosses he hated, all with the promise of leisure at the end. But when retirement finally came, his body was already too frail to travel, his energy too spent to pursue the hobbies he had postponed. He sat in a chair by the window, staring at the world outside, and whispered to me, "I thought I'd have time." The bars had always been there, but he only noticed them once the door had sealed behind him. His cage was built from deferred dreams, and by the time he realized it, the dreams had already expired.

History is filled with such stories. Whole generations who believed they were building security, only to discover they had been building their own prisons. In the company towns of the industrial age, workers traded decades for wages that barely sustained them, comforted by the idea that one day their children would be better off. But many died young, lungs blackened from the mines or bodies broken by machines. Their loyalty had not bought freedom; it had bought an early grave. The door was closed long before they saw it coming.

I once spoke to a woman who stayed in a loveless marriage for thirty-five years. She told herself it was for the children, for the stability, for the respect of her community. She repeated these reasons until they sounded like virtues. But when her children were grown and gone, when the house was quiet, she found herself sitting across from a stranger she no longer loved. She whispered that she had thought about leaving countless times, but each year the possibility seemed smaller, the risks larger. By the time she admitted the truth to herself, she was in her sixties. "I wasted my life," she said, her voice shaking. It wasn't said in anger but in sorrow. She had mistaken captivity for duty, and now the years she might have escaped were gone.

The cruelest thing about realizing the door has closed is the way time distorts around you. At first, you think you have forever. You believe you'll chase your dream once the kids are older, once you've paid off the debt, once the timing is right. The word once becomes a lullaby. You repeat it until the decades vanish. Then suddenly, you wake up and realize that "once" has become "never." Time has passed not in leaps but in tiny, almost imperceptible increments. A thousand small delays added up to a lifetime of waiting.

The trap tightens because of how humans perceive loss. Psychologists call it the sunk cost fallacy — the tendency to keep investing in something because you've already invested so much. People stay in careers they despise because they've already spent years climbing. They stay in marriages that hurt them because they've already built decades together. They stay in places that suffocate them because moving would make all the past sacrifices seem wasted. The irony is that the longer you stay, the more impossible it feels to leave. By the time you realize the past is gone, the future is too.

I once met a man who had wanted to be a painter. In his twenties, he set aside the dream to take a "temporary" office job. He told himself he'd save money first, then pursue art once he was secure. The years passed. Promotions came, along with bigger paychecks, a mortgage, and a family. He told himself he would paint once the kids were older, once the house was paid off, once retirement came. When I met him, he was seventy, his hands trembling too badly to hold a brush. His canvases remained blank, stacked in a dusty corner. "I thought I had more time," he said. The door had closed long before his body failed him. It had closed the day he decided to wait.

What makes these realizations so haunting is how ordinary they are. They aren't stories of dramatic collapse, of sudden imprisonment. They are stories of small choices accumulating into finality. Every "not yet" becomes another turn of the key, every rationalization another bolt in the door. By the time you look up, the room has no exits. The cage wasn't built overnight. It was built one quiet compromise at a time.

What makes the moment of realization unbearable is not only that the door has closed but that you were the one who kept hesitating to walk through it. Nobody forced you to stay. There were no armed guards, no iron gates. You stayed because it felt easier, safer, more respectable. You told yourself there would always be time later. The guilt that comes with this realization is heavier than the bars themselves.

I once visited a relative who had dreamed of becoming a musician. In his twenties, he had played in bands, written songs, and performed in bars. But when marriage and children arrived, he told himself he needed to be practical. He took a stable job and put the guitar in the closet. "Just for now," he told himself. Decades later, when I asked him if he ever regretted it, he nodded without hesitation. "Every day," he said. His hands still moved restlessly, as if they remembered chords his mind had forgotten. He had provided for his family, earned the respect of his neighbors, and built a reputation as a steady man. But behind his eyes was grief for a life unlived. The cage was not only closed — it was sealed with his own signature.

The harsh truth is that many people only admit their captivity when they no longer have the strength to fight it. Bodies wear down, opportunities shrink, the imagination stiffens. A dream that once felt possible now feels embarrassing, childish, irresponsible. The older you get, the more you hear yourself say, "It's too late." And eventually, it is. The cage doesn't close around your circumstances. It closes around your sense of identity. You no longer see yourself as someone who could escape. You see yourself as someone who was always meant to stay.

History is lined with cautionary tales of this transformation. Farmers who tilled the same land generation after generation, not because they loved it, but because they couldn't imagine leaving. Women who spent their lives raising children for men who never valued them, convinced that duty was destiny. Soldiers who marched into battle after battle, sacrificing themselves for causes that evaporated when leaders changed. Their cages were not made of steel. They were made of time. By the time the door shut, it was not that they couldn't leave. It was that leaving no longer made sense.

I remember reading about a factory worker who, on the day the plant finally closed, stood outside the gates with tears in his eyes. For thirty years, he had said he would leave "soon." He would find a better job, move to a better town, and start a new life. But the plant outlasted his ambition. When the gates closed for good, he realized he had been waiting for freedom that never arrived. Now, with no savings and no prospects, he stood outside staring at the rusted fence. The door had not only closed — it had been welded shut.

The tragedy of waiting too long is that regret can't undo anything. You can see the shape of the life you wanted, but you can no longer step into it. You can imagine the road not taken, but your body will not walk it. Regret is a mirror that shows you both who you were and who you could have been. And once you see that reflection, you cannot unsee it.

Yet even in these late realizations, there is something worth paying attention to. The clarity of regret can become a warning for those who still have time. When the elderly whisper their sorrows, when they confess their lives were spent in cages they never escaped, they are not only lamenting. They are testifying.

They are saying to anyone who will listen: don't wait. Don't assume you'll have time later. Don't mistake the open door for a permanent invitation. Doors close, sometimes slowly, sometimes suddenly, but always sooner than you think.

The cruelty of a closed door is that it doesn't announce itself with a bang. There's no moment of dramatic finality, no voice declaring that you've run out of chances. It closes in silence, in increments, until you wake one morning and realize the hinges have rusted shut. You don't remember when it happened, only that it did. By then, the only thing left is memory — and memory is a brutal companion when it's filled with missed exits.

I once sat with an elderly man who had worked in sales his whole life. He had been good at it, respected by colleagues, admired for his persistence. But when I asked him if he was proud of what he had built, he shook his head. "I don't even know what I sold," he said. "Products came and went. I spent forty years talking people into things they didn't need." He had earned a pension, bought a house, and raised a family. From the outside, it looked like success. But in his voice was the flatness of someone who had realized too late that his work had never meant anything to him. He had traded decades for stability, and in the end, the stability felt hollow. The door had closed not on opportunity, but on meaning.

This is the essence of many closed doors: they aren't simply about lost chances. They are about lost selves. Every year you stay in the wrong place, a version of you dies. The young, curious self who wanted adventure. The bold self who wanted to take risks. The creative self who wanted to make something beautiful.

They wither slowly as you convince yourself to be responsible, sensible, and mature. And when you finally realize the door is closed, it is not only freedom that's gone — it is the person you might have been.

Cultures reinforce this quiet death. They celebrate anniversaries of endurance: fifty years in the same marriage, forty years in the same company, generations in the same town. These milestones are framed as triumphs, as proof of loyalty and perseverance. And sometimes they are. But often they are monuments to lives that could have been larger, richer, freer. Behind the applause is the silence of people who wonder what might have happened if they had walked away when the door was still open.

I think about the stories told by hospice workers, who often hear the confessions of the dying. Rarely do people say, "I wish I had worked more." Rarely do they say, "I wish I had stayed longer in situations that drained me." What they say instead is haunting in its consistency: "I wish I had taken more risks. I wish I had said yes to adventure. I wish I had left sooner." These are the voices of people who saw the cage clearly at the very end, when nothing could be done about it. They had lived as though doors would always be there, only to discover that doors, once shut, rarely reopen.

One woman I spoke to in her final weeks confessed she had always wanted to write a book. She had carried the idea inside her for decades, but never started, always waiting for a better moment. Now, lying in bed with machines keeping her alive, she shook her head and said, "I waited too long." There was no bitterness in her tone, only resignation. She didn't lack ideas. She lacked time. The door had closed on her voice, and with it, the chance for the world to ever hear what she had to say.

The tragedy of these stories is that they are not rare. They are everywhere, whispered in quiet conversations, confessed in moments of vulnerability. Most people are too ashamed to admit them out loud, because to do so would reveal how much of their life was lived in waiting. But if you listen closely — to relatives, to neighbors, to strangers — you hear the same refrain again and again: I thought I'd have more time. It is the most common epitaph of a closed door.

What makes the finality of closed doors so painful is the sense of inevitability that comes with them. At first, regret is sharp and frantic. You imagine what you might still salvage, the ways you could claw back what was lost. But the longer you sit with it, the more it hardens into something colder. The realization that no matter what you do, the opportunity has passed. The years you might have used are gone. The self you might have been is gone. The road you might have taken no longer exists.

I once visited a retired teacher who told me she had always dreamed of traveling. She had maps pinned to her wall, magazines filled with destinations she had circled. Every summer, she told herself she would go. But then summer would fill with chores, with family visits, with the inertia of habit. "Next year," she would say. When she finally retired, she planned her first trip — and her health collapsed. She couldn't walk long distances, couldn't climb stairs, and couldn't carry luggage. The dream was still alive in her mind, but her body could no longer follow. She said softly, "I waited too long." Her voice wasn't bitter. It was hollow. She hadn't been robbed. She had simply delayed until the delay itself became a prison.

This is how most cages close — not with violence, but with postponement. The word later is the deadliest in the language of captivity. Later becomes next year, then next decade, then never. The illusion is that you are choosing to wait, that you are in control. But time is the most merciless captor of all. It doesn't pause for your readiness. It doesn't care about your plans. And by the time you realize this, you are out of currency. You cannot buy back the years you spent hesitating.

Even systems are designed this way. Retirement, for example, is framed as freedom deferred. Work hard now, they say, and one day you'll enjoy yourself. But this promise works only if your health, energy, and relationships survive intact. Too often, they don't. The body breaks. Friendships fade. Curiosity dulls. The retirement years arrive, but the version of you who once dreamed of them is already gone. The door is technically open, but you are no longer the person who could walk through it.

The same logic applies to love. I met a man who admitted, in his seventies, that he had loved someone once but had been too afraid to leave his marriage for her. "I thought there would be another chance," he said. "I thought the moment would come back." But the moment never returned. He had stayed put, telling himself it was loyalty, when in truth it was fear. Decades later, he could still see her face in his mind. He didn't cry when he told me. He simply looked at the floor, shaking his head. The door had closed not with a slam, but with silence.

This is why the stories of the dying strike such a chord. They strip away the illusions that keep us quiet in middle age. When people are young, they believe there will always be more time. When they are older, they believe the time they have already spent makes it too late to change. Only at the very end do they realize both beliefs were lies. The truth is simpler and harsher: the only time you have is now, and once it's gone, it is gone forever.

I remember an interview with a hospice nurse who said the most common regret she heard was not about failure but about hesitation. People rarely regretted risks they had taken, even when those risks had gone badly. They regretted the risks they hadn't taken. They regretted the words they hadn't said, the doors they hadn't walked through, the lives they had postponed until it was too late. "If only I had tried," they whispered. "If only I hadn't waited." Their cages had never been locked. They had simply convinced themselves the timing wasn't right. And then the timing vanished.

The lesson is brutal, but it is also liberating: doors do not stay open forever. They close, sometimes slowly, sometimes suddenly, but always sooner than you think. To recognize this is to strip the illusion of safety from the word later. Later is a gamble, and the odds are rarely in your favor.

When the door is already closed, there is nothing left but testimony. Those who see it at the end become witnesses, their voices carrying warnings for those who still have time. If you listen, you hear the pattern clearly: don't wait. Don't mistake hesitation for caution. Don't confuse duty with destiny. Don't let pride or loyalty keep you still until time chooses you. The stories of closed doors are not tragedies. They are maps drawn in reverse. They tell you where not to go, what not to postpone, and what not to sacrifice.

Freedom is not infinite. It is not permanent. It is not waiting for you at the end of a career, or at the end of a contract, or in some distant future when the timing will be better. Freedom is fragile, fleeting, and perishable. And the only way to keep the door from closing is to walk through it before it does.

Chapter 5: Naming the Cage

Every prison has a name. The walls may be invisible, the bars disguised as duty or comfort, but until you can call them what they are, you cannot see them clearly enough to escape. Language is the first act of rebellion. To name the cage is to strip away the illusion that it is simply "life" or "the way things are." Once you name it, you expose it, and once exposed, it begins to weaken.

Most people don't realize how many cages they live in because they have never learned to distinguish one from another. They feel restless, anxious, and suffocated, but they don't know why. They blame themselves, assuming it must be personal weakness. But the problem is not always inside them. Often, it is structural, cultural, or relational. It is the weight of a trap that has never been identified. Naming is how you turn suffocation into something you can fight.

The first and most obvious cage is financial. Money is supposed to liberate — that's the story we're told. Earn enough and you can buy freedom. But most people discover that the pursuit of money becomes its own trap. Debt pulls the bars tight. Mortgages stretch into decades. Credit cards bleed in silence. Even success hardens into captivity: the bigger the salary, the more people chain themselves to jobs they hate because they can't imagine walking away from the paycheck. I knew a man who once turned down a dream opportunity because it paid less than his current role. He told me, "I can't afford to take a step back." What he didn't see was that he was already caged — his income had become his prison, gilded but binding all the same.

Then there are emotional cages, the kind built from guilt, fear, or shame. These traps are invisible because they look like feelings rather than structures. A daughter stays close to parents who diminish her because she fears disappointing them. A man swallows his truth about who he loves because shame has welded bars around him. A friend stays in relationships that no longer nourish them because guilt whispers that leaving would be betrayal. These cages don't rely on paperwork or penalties. They rely on the human heart's ability to turn tenderness into chains.

Relational cages are close cousins, forged not by emotion but by the expectations of others. Families that demand obedience. Partners who punish independence. Friends who ridicule ambition. A woman I once knew turned down a job in another city because her friends mocked her for "thinking she was better than everyone." She laughed it off at the time, but decades later, she admitted the bitterness had never left. The cage was not geography but permission. She had tied her life to the crowd's approval, and the crowd locked the door.

Cognitive cages are subtler still. These are traps of perception, the habits of thought that keep people captive even when the door is wide open. Denial is one — the refusal to admit the bars exist, the constant insistence that things are fine. Another is the safety story, the belief that stability is always wiser than risk. Then there is the crowd effect, the mental reflex that convinces you that what everyone else is doing must be correct. These cognitive patterns are so ingrained that they rarely feel like choices. They feel like the truth. But they are simply the brain's way of keeping you docile.

Finally, there are systemic cages — the broad structures that catch entire populations. Laws, economies, institutions. A person may believe they are free, but their options are shaped by policies they never voted for, corporations they never agreed to serve, histories they never lived but inherited all the same. The worker is locked into an exploitative industry. The immigrant navigating borders designed to exclude them. The citizen whose vote is drowned in systems tilted against them. These cages are vast and impersonal, but no less real. They create the environment in which every personal cage is reinforced.

Each of these categories — financial, emotional, relational, cognitive, systemic — has its own flavor, its own rules. Some overlap, feeding into one another until you can't tell where one ends and another begins. Debt fuels emotional shame. Pride fuels relational traps. Systems reinforce denial. The cages stack and interlock until escape feels impossible. But simpler: they are only impossible when they remain unnamed.

Once you begin naming cages, the world looks different. The job you once called secure now looks like a financial leash. The relationship you called loyalty now feels like dependency. The routines you thought of as stability reveal themselves as stagnation. Naming doesn't immediately free you, but it does something as important: it breaks the spell of inevitability. You stop saying, "This is the way life is," and start saying, "This is a trap." That shift in language is a power shift.

I knew a woman who lived under what she called family duty. She cared for her aging parents, raised her siblings' children when they faltered, and ran errands for relatives who leaned on her constantly. For years, she told herself she was being noble. But one night she admitted, with exhaustion dripping from her voice, "I don't have a life of my own." That sentence was her act of naming. She stopped calling it duty and started calling it what it was: captivity dressed as obligation. Nothing changed overnight, but within a year, she had drawn boundaries that once seemed impossible. She had not broken free yet, but she had loosened the bars.

Financial cages often resist naming because they are socially reinforced. Debt is normalized. Mortgages are celebrated. People boast about the square footage of their homes while hiding the decades of payments chained to their names. A man I once met introduced himself by saying, "I'm a homeowner." His chest swelled with pride. But when he explained his situation, it became clear that the bank owned his house, not him. He was renting it from them for thirty years under the illusion of ownership. When I said this aloud, his smile faltered. He had never thought of it that way. Naming shattered the illusion. He was proud, but pride had blinded him to his so-called asset was also his prison.

Relational cages carry similar blind spots. People defend them fiercely because the cost of questioning them is high. To admit that a friendship has become toxic, or that a family bond is suffocating, feels like betrayal. But betrayal is sometimes the word the cage itself uses to defend its existence. A man once told me he could never move away from his hometown because his parents would see it as abandonment. He repeated the word with guilt: abandonment. When I asked if he thought he owed his entire life to their expectations, he went silent. That silence was the sound of a cage being named. For the first time, he realized his loyalty was not devotion but captivity.

Cognitive cages are even harder to identify because they disguise themselves as reason. Denial is framed as optimism. Following the crowd is framed as wisdom. Playing it safe is framed as maturity. But these are simply thought patterns designed to keep you in place. I once worked with someone who kept insisting their job was "fine." They said it so often it sounded rehearsed. But when pressed, their eyes darted, their voice thinned, and finally they admitted, "I hate it here." The difference between "fine" and "hate" was the difference between denial and truth. The cage had been there all along, invisible until they dared to name it.

Systemic cages demand an even sharper eye, because they are designed to be invisible. Most people don't question the structure of the economy they live in, or the laws that govern their mobility, or the culture that shapes their desires. They assume the playing field is natural. But the moment you say, "This system is a trap," you pull it into the light. Think of workers in factories that shutter without warning, entire towns collapsing overnight. They realize too late that the "opportunity" they had been promised was a leash. Systems profit from your blindness. Naming them makes them tremble.

To name a cage is not to escape it. But it is the beginning of escape. Once you can call your prison by its true name, you stop confusing it with life. You stop defending it as responsibility, love, or maturity. You begin to see it as a structure with limits, not as a natural law. And once you see limits, you begin to imagine ways around them. Language does not open the door, but it puts the key in your hand.

He power of naming lies not only in clarity but in courage. To call something a trap is to admit that you have been deceived. That admission stings. Nobody wants to confess they have spent years in cages of their own making or cages they allowed others to build around them. So people resist naming because naming is humiliating. It strips away the comforting illusions. But only through humiliation can liberation begin.

I once spoke to a man who described himself as a "provider." He wore the word like armor. He worked long hours, sacrificed weekends, aged before his time, all in the name of providing for his family. But when his children grew older, they admitted quietly that they barely saw him, that they had wished for his presence more than his paychecks. For years, he had defended his exhaustion as proof of love. But when he finally admitted the truth, he said it in a whisper: "I worked myself into a cage." That was the moment he named it. Provider was not free. Provider was a trap disguised as virtue.

These disguises are everywhere. The student drowning in loans says they are "investing in their future." The spouse who stays in a dead marriage says they are "keeping the family together." The employee stuck in a toxic job says they are "being responsible." Each phrase is a mask that makes the cage easier to bear. But once you name the mask, you cannot unsee it. "Investment" is debt. "Family unity" is entrapment.

"Responsibility" is inertia. Naming punctures the mask and reveals the bars.

What frightens people most about naming is that it creates obligation. Once you admit something is a cage, you can no longer pretend to be free. You can no longer tell yourself that things are fine or that you are choosing to stay. The illusion evaporates, and you are left with a choice: remain knowingly captive, or begin the messy, terrifying work of escape. Many people would rather stay blind. Blindness is easier. Truth demands action.

I remember a woman who once told me she could never leave her city because her entire network was there. She repeated the words like a mantra: "Everything I need is here." But one night she confessed she had always wanted to move abroad, to live differently. When I asked why she didn't, she said quietly, "Because then I'd have to admit I've been lying to myself all these years." Her cage was not geography. It was the fear of exposure. To name her dream was to name her captivity, and she wasn't ready to face either.

Systemic cages often force the hardest reckonings. A worker in an underpaid industry may know, deep down, that the system is rigged against them. But to say it aloud is to admit that their sacrifice, their decades of labor, their belief in meritocracy was misplaced. It is easier to stay silent, to keep repeating that hard work pays off, than to admit the bars were always there. This is why societies cling so tightly to myths of opportunity. They are masks that prevent the masses from naming the system itself as a cage. And when people do name it, upheaval begins. Revolutions start not with violence but with language. Someone dares to say: we are not free. And once that sentence spreads, the walls tremble.

The act of naming also brings precision. Financial cages are not "being broke." They are debt spirals, predatory contracts, golden handcuffs that look like prosperity. Emotional cages are not "feeling bad." They are guilt loops, shame cycles, fear scripts that repeat until they become identity. Relational cages are not "family obligations." They are obligations enforced by ridicule, withdrawal, or punishment. Cognitive cages are not "thinking errors." They are denial systems, conformity pressures, and safety stories that masquerade as wisdom. Systemic cages are not "the way the world works." They are intentional structures designed to keep certain people in place and others in power. Precision matters because only when you can describe the cage in detail can you begin to dismantle it.

Every time I've seen someone escape, it started with a sentence. A worker saying, "This isn't stability, this is exploitation." A spouse saying, "This isn't love, this is fear." A student saying, "This isn't opportunity, this is indenture." The moment those words leave their mouths, the bars lose a fraction of their strength. Nothing material has changed, but the story has. And stories are the architecture of cages. Change the story, and the cage begins to collapse.

The act of naming doesn't reveal traps. It forces you to confront the choices that have been shaped by them. When you say, "This is a financial cage," you can no longer treat endless overtime as ambition. When you say, "This is an emotional cage," you can no longer call guilt devotion. When you say, "This is a cognitive cage," you can no longer dismiss denial as optimism. Naming makes excuses impossible. And without excuses, unavoidable: you are not living freely.

I once listened to a man describe his career. He had risen steadily, earning promotions, buying bigger houses, climbing a ladder he believed was leading somewhere important. But one day, over drinks, he admitted that every step up had also been a step deeper inside. His title was grand, his pay generous, but he whispered that he felt hollow. "I can't leave," he said, "but I don't want to stay." For the first time, he called it what it was: a trap of status. His pride had built it, and his fear kept him there. The moment he named it, he looked terrified. But beneath the terror was a flicker of relief. He finally had words for the bars he had felt pressing against him for years.

That relief is part of the paradox. Naming is painful, but it also carries liberation. Even if you do nothing right away, the simple act of calling something a cage changes the relationship. You are no longer unconscious. You are no longer complicit without awareness. You have a choice now, and choice is dangerous to any trap.

Denial, crowd, and safety — the trio of cognitive tricks — often unravel first once they are named. Denial collapses when you say aloud, "I hate this." The crowd loses its grip when you whisper, "Just because everyone does it doesn't mean it's right." Safety dissolves when you admit, "This isn't safety. This is stagnation." Each small sentence becomes a crack. You might not act immediately, but you can't go back to blindness. Once you have named the cage, the old defenses no longer fit.

Cultures fear this process because it spreads. One person calls their situation captivity, and others begin to see their own. I've seen it happen in workplaces where one employee quits and names the company for what it is — toxic, exploitative. Suddenly, conversations shift. Others whisper their own doubts. Some begin to plan their own exits. The cage relies on silence. Naming is contagious noise.

The same is true in families. One person breaks from tradition, calls the obligations suffocating, and dares to leave. At first, they are branded selfish, ungrateful. But later, when others see their life blossom, the accusations soften. Sometimes, younger members follow. One person's naming gives another the courage to speak. This is why cages are defended so fiercely — not because they are unbreakable, but because one escape weakens the whole illusion.

The most difficult cages to name are systemic ones, because they implicate not only individuals but entire ways of living. To say "this economy is a trap" threatens every story people have told themselves about progress and prosperity. To say "this system is rigged" challenges the legitimacy of authority itself. People who dare to name systemic cages are often punished, ostracized, and silenced. But their naming is the first step toward collective escape. Revolutions don't begin with weapons. They begin with words: slavery, exploitation, and oppression. Every great movement started with someone naming the bars everyone else had been trained not to see.

But naming isn't enough. Without action, it curdles into bitterness. People who identify their cages but never move beyond them often become the most cynical of all, pointing out traps everywhere while refusing to test their own bars. Naming is only the first cut — the knife that opens possibilities. What you do with it determines whether you stay bitter or break free.

I think of all the people who carry secret sentences in their heads. "I hate my job." "I don't love my partner." "I can't breathe in this town." These words repeat in silence, whispered at night, muttered on long commutes, scribbled in journals. They are names waiting to be spoken aloud. And the moment they are, something changes. The room tilts. The air shifts. The cage loses a fraction of its authority. The sentence itself becomes a seed of escape.

Naming the cage doesn't end captivity. But it ends the illusion that captivity is freedom. And that may be the most important step of all. Because once you see the difference, once you hear yourself say it, once you have language for your chains, you can no longer polish them with pride. You can no longer call them safe. You can no longer decorate them with loyalty. You can only face them for what they are: bars.

Every chapter of escape begins with a sentence. The courage to name the cage is the courage to begin.

ACT TWO

Chapter 6: Escape Thinking

The first step in breaking out of any cage is not physical but mental. You cannot saw through bars if your head is still convinced they are unbreakable. Escape begins with a shift in perspective so small it almost looks trivial from the outside, yet it is revolutionary for the person who makes it. It is the shift from asking "How do I survive here?" to asking "How do I get out of here?" That single reframing changes the entire geometry of the mind.

Most people never make it. They spend their lives refining strategies of survival inside their traps. They learn how to manage debt instead of dismantling it, how to cope with toxic relationships instead of leaving them, how to tolerate work they despise instead of walking away. They become experts at adaptation, masters of endurance. Their skill is impressive, but it is a skill invested in the wrong direction. They are polishing their cages instead of plotting escape.

I knew a man who prided himself on being able to handle anything his job threw at him. The hours grew longer, the pressure harsher, but he added each time. He learned breathing techniques, kept motivational quotes taped to his monitor, and even started jogging at dawn to stay sharp. His colleagues admired his resilience. But when I asked him what all this effort was for, he had no answer. He wasn't working toward freedom.

He was working toward the ability to stay longer in captivity. That is the trap of survival thinking — you become good at living in places you should never have stayed in the first place.

Escape thinking doesn't begin with elaborate plans. It begins with questions. What if I refused to play by these rules? What if I left instead of staying? What if I treated this system not as permanent but as temporary? These questions are dangerous because they pierce the story you've been telling yourself about inevitability. They open a crack in the wall. And once a crack appears, the mind can't help but peer through it.

I once met a woman who had worked in the same office for twenty years. She was respected, steady, and predictable. But one afternoon she said quietly, "I started asking myself what would happen if I walked out and didn't come back." The thought shocked her. It felt almost obscene. But once it arrived, it wouldn't leave. Each morning as she entered, the question echoed: What if you didn't? That single question became unbearable until one day she answered it. She quit without another job lined up, terrified but alive. Later, she told me it was the most important question she had ever asked.

Escape thinking is contrarian by nature. It refuses the stories that culture repeats like scripture. Where survival thinking asks how to be loyal, escape thinking asks whether loyalty is deserved. Where survival thinking asks how to make the paycheck stretch, escape thinking asks whether the paycheck itself is worth the life it costs. Where survival thinking clings to safety, escape thinking wonders if safety is another word for stagnation. The questions are dangerous because they strip away the camouflage. They reveal the cage for what it is, and once revealed, it becomes harder to ignore.

The first time you think like this, your body rebels. Fear rushes in, inertia pulls hard, loyalty screams betrayal. You imagine the disasters that will follow if you step out of line. But fear always arrives dressed in exaggeration. It insists you'll be ruined, shunned, and alone. Most of the time, what happens is smaller. People grumble. You lose some money. You disappoint someone. You face uncertainty. These costs are real, but they are not annihilation. The mind paints catastrophe to keep you still, because stillness is easier than movement. Escape thinking begins when you recognize this exaggeration for what it is: the bar's bluffing.

I knew another man who wanted to move across the country to pursue work he loved, but fear convinced him that leaving his hometown would mean losing everyone. "I'd have no one," he told me. But when he finally left, the reality was different. Some people drifted away. Others visited. He made new connections faster than he imagined. The catastrophe never came. The bars had looked solid, but when he pushed, they bent. The cost was real, but not fatal. That is the secret fear never tells you: escape hurts, but captivity kills slowly.

Escape thinking is not reckless. It is not about burning bridges for the thrill of watching them collapse. It is about clarity. It asks: Is this situation survivable but suffocating? If so, why am I spending my life surviving instead of living? Escape thinking refuses to mistake endurance for strength. Strength is walking away. Endurance is polishing chains. One frees you, the other only makes captivity more comfortable.

The hardest part of cultivating escape thinking is enduring the criticism that comes with it. People invested in their own cages will call you reckless, selfish, and immature. They will point to your doubts as proof of irresponsibility. This is not because your questions are wrong. It is because your questions threaten their equilibrium. If you can leave, then maybe they could too — and that possibility terrifies them. Criticism is the price of freedom. To think of escape is to accept that you will not be applauded for it, at least not at first.

Escape begins in imagination. Not in blueprints, not in logistics, not in maps. Imagination. You have to be able to picture yourself outside, even if the picture is blurry. You have to let your mind run down paths you've been taught to dismiss as impossible. What if I started over? What if I walked away? What if I refused? These thoughts are dangerous because they awaken possibilities. And possibility, once awakened, is difficult to put back to sleep.

The imagination of escape doesn't show you the door. It begins to make the walls thinner. What once felt like immovable structures start to look like habits, and habits can be broken. The mortgage you thought of as permanent is suddenly numbers on paper. The job you thought was irreplaceable reveals itself as one of millions. The relationship you thought you couldn't survive without starts to look like something you already survived years ago. Nothing outside has changed yet, but inside, the weight shifts. You begin to see that most traps rely not on strength but on your willingness to treat them as eternal.

The great lie of captivity is that your life is too entangled to move. Escape thinking asks whether that entanglement is real or assumed. I once spoke with a woman who said she couldn't leave her job because she was "locked in by bills." But when she looked closely, she realized half her bills came from things she didn't need—subscriptions, conveniences, symbols of a life she didn't even enjoy. She canceled them, and suddenly her monthly expenses shrank. The bars she thought were welded steel were paper-thin. She wasn't locked in by necessity. She was locked in by assumption.

This is one of the most startling discoveries for anyone who shifts into escape thinking: how much of the trap is self-maintained. People cling to possessions, to titles, to routines, telling themselves these things are indispensable. But when they are stripped away—by crisis, by chance, by choice—the person realizes they were never essential at all. The fear of losing them was heavier than the loss itself. This is why escape often looks reckless from the outside. The onlookers are still carrying the weight of illusions that the escapee has already dropped.

But imagination alone is not enough. Escape thinking must evolve into an experiment. Small tests, subtle rebellions, acts of refusal. The person who always says yes tries saying no once. The worker who never leaves on time walks out at five o'clock sharp. The spouse who swallows every feeling speaks a single forbidden truth. These experiments don't free anyone completely, but they prove something critical: the world doesn't end when you defy the rules. The cage rattles, but it doesn't collapse on top of you. This is how people discover that the bars are not as lethal as they seemed.

I knew a man who decided to stop answering emails after dinner. It sounds trivial, but for him it was revolutionary. For years, he had treated his phone like a leash, responding instantly to his boss at all hours. The night he ignored a message, he felt sick with fear. He imagined reprimands, demotion, disaster. But nothing happened. His boss sent another message in the morning, no different from before. That one act of refusal changed him. He realized how much of his captivity had been voluntary. He had trained himself to obey. Now, with one small act of rebellion, he began retraining himself to resist.

Escape thinking thrives on these experiments because they build evidence. Fear always predicts catastrophe. Experiment proves otherwise. Every small act of disobedience creates a file of proof in the mind: you can push against the bars and survive. Over time, the file grows thick. The mind that once whispered "impossible" begins to whisper "maybe." And "maybe" is the most dangerous word a cage can hear.

This is why many systems work so hard to prevent even small acts of defiance. Companies punish workers for leaving early, not because the hours matter, but because the precedent does. Families shame members who step out of line, not because one decision destroys tradition, but because it threatens to expose the tradition as optional. Systems don't fear collapse from one person walking away. They fear the contagion of possibility. If one person leaves, others may follow. Escape thinking spreads like fire.

Yet the first sparks of escape thinking can be agonizing to live with. Once you've seen the bars, you can't unsee them. The job you tolerated yesterday feels unbearable today. The relationship you rationalized last week feels suffocating this week. Awareness increases the pressure. Some people mistake this for failure. They think: I was happier before I questioned things. But that's an illusion. They weren't happier. They were anesthetized. Escape thinking removes the anesthetic. It hurts, but the pain is proof of awakening.

The most dangerous moment is when you are caught between cages and freedom—when you've named the trap, imagined the door, but haven't yet walked through. This is the liminal space where many people turn back. They feel the pressure, the anxiety, the uncertainty, and decide it's easier to stay where they were. But those who endure the discomfort find that the liminal space is also where the real transformation happens. You are no longer the old self, but not yet the new one. It is in this tension that a resolution is forged.

I once knew a woman who decided to leave her marriage after years of silence. She packed her things, signed a lease, and for the first few weeks lived in a state of panic. She doubted herself constantly. She cried in the middle of the night. She almost went back. But she stayed through the discomfort, and eventually the panic gave way to peace. She told me later, "The hardest part wasn't leaving. It was surviving the space right after." Escape thinking is not a clean leap. It is a trembling, painful passage through uncertainty. But on the other side is air you didn't realize you had been missing.

The crucial truth is this: escape doesn't start with the door opening. It starts with the decision that staying is no longer acceptable. The door may not be visible yet. The plan may not be formed. The risks may be enormous. But the refusal to keep surviving in captivity is itself the beginning of freedom. Once you decide you will not stay, the mind begins to look for exits where before it saw only walls. The questions sharpen. The experiments grow bolder. The cracks widen. And then, almost inevitably, the door appears.

The hardest truth about escape thinking is that once it takes root, you can no longer live comfortably in captivity. The cage may still surround you, but the illusion that it is tolerable is gone. You notice the fluorescent hum of the office lights in a way you never did before. You feel the weight of the wedding ring that once felt like security but now feels like a shackle. You count the hours of your commute and realize you are not moving toward life but away from it. The mind that has glimpsed freedom becomes restless, and restlessness is dangerous to the status quo.

Restlessness is often pathologized. Doctors call it anxiety. Employers call it dissatisfaction. Families call it rebellion. And sometimes it is all of those things. But it is also the natural signal of awakening. To feel restless is to feel the tension between the life you are living and the life you know is possible. It is not a flaw to be medicated out of existence. It is a flare shot from the soul, signaling that the cage is no longer invisible.

I knew a man who suddenly found himself unable to sleep before work. For years, he had followed the same routine without complaint. Then, almost overnight, dread filled him every Sunday evening. His chest tightened, his stomach turned, his mind replayed every miserable moment of the week ahead. His doctor told him it was stress. His wife told him to tough it out. But what it was was awareness. He had begun to see the bars. His body was sounding the alarm his mind had ignored. Within a year, he left the job. The dread vanished. The restlessness had been his compass, pointing not toward collapse but toward freedom.

Escape thinking reframes this restlessness not as a symptom but as a guide. The anxiety you feel in the presence of certain people, the heaviness in your chest when you step into a certain building, the exhaustion that follows particular obligations — these are not random inconveniences. They are signals. The cage broadcasts its presence through the body. Survival thinking tells you to ignore them, to medicate them, to muscle through. Escape thinking tells you to listen closely. The discomfort is not the problem. The cage is.

But to listen to the body is dangerous in a culture that thrives on ignoring it. Capitalism depends on people overriding fatigue to keep working, overriding loneliness to keep consuming, overriding intuition to keep obeying. The moment you start treating your body's discomfort as truth, you begin to undermine the entire system. Your refusal to numb yourself is an act of sabotage. To listen to your restlessness is to begin plotting escape.

The next step in escape thinking is clarity about cost. Every cage will tell you that leaving is too expensive. You will lose money, reputation, and comfort. And it's true — there is always a price. But what survival thinking hides from you is that there is also a cost to staying. The years you trade. The health you erode. The dreams you abandon. Captivity is not free. It charges interest on every sacrifice, compounding quietly until the bill arrives in the form of regret.

I once spoke to a woman who stayed in a relationship long after it had died. She told herself leaving would be too painful, too disruptive. She feared financial strain, social judgment, and the anger of her partner. And when she finally left, all those costs were real. But what struck her most was the realization that staying had been even more expensive. "I lost years," she said. "Years I can't get back." The bars had been priced not in dollars but in time, and time was the one currency she could never replenish.

Escape thinking forces this calculation into the open. It asks not only, "What will it cost me to leave?" but also, "What is it costing me to stay?" Once both sides of the ledger are visible, captivity begins to look far less affordable. The illusions of stability collapse when you realize that stability is eating you alive.

This is why escape thinking is not reckless but rational. The reckless ones are those who never do the math, who keep paying the hidden costs until the bill arrives too late to act. Escape thinkers are accountants of the soul. They add up the lost time, the drained energy, the crushed dreams, and they recognize that leaving, however costly, is cheaper than staying.

Yet clarity is not enough. Many people see the math clearly and still hesitate. This is because escape thinking requires courage to step into uncertainty. The cage may be painful, but at least it is familiar. The world outside is unknown, and the unknown is terrifying. The only way through is to expand your tolerance for uncertainty. To accept that freedom is not comfort. It is exposure, risk, vulnerability. And to decide that these are better than the certainty of slow death inside.

I once knew a man who left a corporate job to start his own business. He confessed later that the first year was hell. He doubted himself constantly. Money was tight, failures frequent. He nearly went back more than once. But when I asked him if he regretted it, his face lit up. "No," he said. "Even when it was hard, it was mine. Every day, it was mine." Escape thinking doesn't promise ease. It promises ownership of your life. That ownership is priceless, and it cannot be rented inside a cage.

The final piece of escape thinking is not optimism but resolve. You don't have to believe everything will work out. You don't have to be sure of success. You only have to be sure that staying is no longer acceptable. That certainty becomes your anchor in the storm. When fear exaggerates, when inertia tempts, when pride shames, when loyalty accuses, you return to the one simple truth: captivity is not an option. From there, every step forward, however uncertain, becomes a step toward life.

Escape thinking is not a one-time revelation but a discipline. It must be practiced, repeated, reinforced, or else the old habits creep back in. The cages are patient. They wait for your exhaustion, your doubt, your longing for comfort. They whisper that maybe survival isn't so bad after all, that maybe you imagined the bars, that maybe the cost of freedom is too high. And if you stop practicing escape thinking, you begin to believe them again. The lock slides back into place, almost without sound.

The discipline begins with refusing old language. You stop calling debt "an investment in the future." You stop calling obligation "duty." You stop calling numbness "stability." Words matter because they are the scaffolding of cages. Tear down the language, and the structure begins to wobble. The world will not help you in this. Friends will insist you are overreacting, colleagues will say you are reckless, and family will call you selfish. But escape thinking requires loyalty to clarity over loyalty to comfort.

It continues with refusal in action. Not dramatic rebellion, not grand gestures, but steady, deliberate acts that affirm your choice. You walk away from conversations that drain you. You decline obligations that suffocate you. You cut ties with possessions that chain you. Each refusal is a brick removed from the wall. Small, yes. But walls fall brick by brick.

Most of all, escape thinking requires remembering the truth you already discovered: captivity costs more than freedom. Whenever doubt creeps in, whenever fear tells you to turn back, you return to the math. You count the years, the dreams, the vitality already spent inside, and you remember that the bill is still running. Freedom may be uncertain, but captivity is fatal.

The mind that practices escape thinking daily begins to change shape. It becomes sharper, hungrier, and more alert to hidden bars. You start to notice cages before you step into them. You recognize the tone of voices that disguise obligation as love, contracts that disguise servitude as opportunity, and traditions that disguise inertia as virtue. You are no longer the same person who accepted cages without question. You have become someone dangerous to captivity.

That is the point. Escape thinking turns you from a prisoner into a threat. Not because you have already broken free, but because you now know that freedom is possible. The cage survives only when you believe it is inevitable. The moment you stop believing, the moment you begin imagining, refusing, recalculating, you become the most dangerous thing a cage can face: someone who has started planning their way out.

Chapter 7: The First Cut is the Deepest

Every escape begins with a wound. You cannot slip out of a cage without leaving something behind, and what you leave almost always bleeds. People fantasize about freedom as a clean break, a graceful exit, a story that can be told without shame or loss. But the reality is harsher. Escape requires sacrifice. The bars don't give way because you asked politely. They give way because you cut through them, and cutting always costs.

The first cut is the deepest because it severs the illusions that kept you safe. Until you act, you can still pretend the cage isn't so bad. You can still imagine you'll leave someday. But once you cut, you destroy that safety net. There is no going back. You have declared war on the bars, and the bars will answer. That is why most people hesitate forever at the edge. They want freedom without cost, escape without pain. They are waiting for a door that opens without resistance. It never comes.

I once met a man who left a secure corporate job to start his own company. From the outside, it looked bold. From the inside, it was agony. He lost his steady paycheck, his professional identity, and the approval of his family, all in one move. He told me that the first year felt like freefall. "I thought I was going to drown," he said. But then his eyes lit up. "It was worth it." The cut had been deep, but it was the price of air.

The cut might be money. Leaving a job, selling possessions, downsizing a lifestyle built on debt. These sacrifices sting because money is more than paper; it is security, status, and permission rolled into one. To cut it is to admit you value freedom over safety, meaning over approval. The world will call you foolish. People will ask how you could walk away from stability. But what they call stability is often gilded captivity. The cut proves you are willing to risk comfort for life.

The cut might be reputation. The person who leaves a respected profession, the spouse who ends a marriage everyone else admired, the friend who breaks from the group. When you sever your reputation, you are cutting away not only others' approval but your own identity. You are burning the mask you once wore. The first time you feel eyes on you with judgment instead of admiration, it burns. You wonder if you made a mistake. But judgment fades. The wound scabs over. What remains is the raw truth of who you are without the mask.

The cut might be relationships. Escape often means walking away from people who cannot or will not understand. Friends who mock you for changing, family who guilt you for leaving, partners who cling to the cage you are determined to break. These cuts are the most painful because they slice through bonds you thought were permanent. But that some relationships exist only to reinforce captivity. When you walk away, you learn which ties were real and which were chains. The chains snap. The ties survive.

The cut might even be identity itself. Many people stay in cages not because of money or others, but because they are afraid of losing the story they tell themselves. The successful lawyer. The loyal spouse. The dependable provider. These stories hold the bars in place. To escape is to kill the story, to admit that you are not who you pretended to be. This is why escape feels like death: you are burying an old self. But in the grave is the seed of someone new.

The first cut is terrifying because it is irreversible. Once you sell the house, once you quit the job, once you speak the forbidden truth, you cannot unsay it. There is no way to retreat into the illusion of comfort. That is why this cut is so powerful. It commits you to the path of escape. You are no longer rehearsing. You are running. And in running, you discover strength you never knew you had.

I knew a woman who left a marriage after thirty years. Everyone around her was shocked. They called her reckless, selfish, and cruel. She wept every night for months. She doubted herself constantly. But she told me later, "I realized the pain of staying had become worse than the pain of leaving." That was the cut. It was brutal, but it was honest. And honesty, she discovered, was worth every tear.

Escape cannot be theoretical forever. At some point, you must cut. That cut will hurt. It will leave scars. But scars are proof that you lived. Scars are the body's memory of freedom won. The first cut is the deepest, and it is also the most necessary. Without it, escape remains a fantasy. With it, the fantasy becomes a path.

The shock of the first cut lingers longer than people expect. You think once you've acted, once you've quit the job, left the marriage, sold the house, the pain will recede. But the wound aches for a long time. It throbs in moments of doubt, flares when you see others still inside their cages, mocks you when the new path feels uncertain. The temptation is to stitch yourself back into the old life, to crawl back through the opening and pretend it never happened. But once you've cut, retreat is an illusion. The old life won't take you back, not. It will always see you as a suspect, tainted by your willingness to leave.

This is why the first cut is the most dangerous. It is not only about loss but about identity. You are no longer who you were, but not yet who you are becoming. That liminal space is dizzying. It feels like freefall. People describe it as depression, panic, and instability. And in a sense, it is all of those things. But it is also a transformation. The skin is sloughing off. The scar tissue is forming. You are in between selves, and that is the rawest place a human can stand.

Society does not know how to deal with people in this state. Employers label them unreliable. Families call them selfish. Friends call them impulsive. But what they are, truly, is dangerous. They have stepped outside the expected script, and scripts are what keep systems running. Once you show that leaving is possible, you destabilize everyone who stayed. Your very existence becomes a challenge. That is why judgment rains down so harshly on those who make the first cut. It isn't about you. It's about the threat you represent to the cages others still accept.

I once knew a man who left a prestigious medical career after realizing he had chosen it to please his parents. He walked away in his mid-thirties, abandoning a path that guaranteed wealth and admiration. His colleagues ridiculed him. His family disowned him. For years, he was treated as a cautionary tale. But he told me later, "I would rather be condemned for leaving than praised for staying." That is the paradox of the first cut. The condemnation hurts, but it also confirms you have broken free from the system of approval that kept you chained.

The pain of the cut also clarifies what matters. When you lose money, you discover whether it was your master or your tool. When you lose reputation, you discover whether identity was borrowed or earned. When you lose relationships, you discover who loved you for yourself and who loved you for your compliance. When you lose an old self, you discover how much of it was costume. Every cut peels away illusions until what remains is raw but real.

There is a strange liberation in this rawness. You no longer have anything to defend. The paycheck is gone, the title discarded, the approval withdrawn. You are stripped bare, and with that stripping comes clarity. You see what cages cost you. You see how much of your energy was spent preserving appearances. You see how fragile the things you thought were solid were. When the wound is open, vision sharpens. Pain becomes a kind of light.

I met a woman who described this moment after she walked away from a church community that had defined her entire life. She said the loneliness was unbearable at first. She lost her friends, her family's respect, even her sense of God. But she also said that in the silence that followed, she discovered her own voice. "For the first time, I knew what I believed," she told me. The cut had cost her almost everything, but what it gave her was something she had never had before: a self not built by others.

The first cut is not meant to be clean. It tears, it scars, it shocks. But in that mess is the truth. If escape were easy, everyone would do it. The difficulty is proving its value. The wound teaches you that freedom is not free, but it is worth the price. And the scar that remains is not shame but memory. It is the body's way of saying: I survived.

Those who never cut live with a different kind of wound. The wound of silence, of regret, of "what if." That wound is invisible but no less real. It festers in the background, leaking into conversations, coloring their view of others. They sneer at risk-takers, mock the restless, dismiss the bold — not because those people are wrong, but because their presence reminds them of the cut they never made. The bitterness of the uncut is one of the saddest sights in the world. They carry their cage inside them until the end.

The lesson is brutal but clear: if you want freedom, you will bleed. There is no clever trick, no smooth path, no painless escape. The first cut is the deepest because it is the one that separates fantasy from reality. Before it, freedom is a dream. After it, freedom is a wound you are willing to tend. And tending it is how you heal into someone new.

There is a reason the first cut feels like betrayal. You are not only severing yourself from the cage but also from the people who remain inside it. To them, your action is not neutral. It is a rebuke. Your refusal to keep playing by the rules forces them to confront that they are still playing. And rather than face that discomfort, they lash out at you.

I once spoke to a man who quit his job in finance because he felt hollow selling futures that destroyed other people's lives. His colleagues mocked him mercilessly. They called him idealistic, naïve, irresponsible. Yet years later, when some of those same colleagues lost their jobs in a market collapse, they admitted privately they envied his decision. Their ridicule had never been about him. It had been about their own inability to cut. That is how the first wound multiplies: it tears not only your skin but theirs.

Families are especially brutal when confronted with the first cut. A daughter leaves the career path chosen for her and is accused of dishonor. A son leaves the religion of his parents and is accused of rebellion. A partner leaves a marriage and is accused of destroying the family. These accusations sting because they are framed as moral failures. But morality is often another lock on the cage. What looks like betrayal from inside the trap is loyalty to life from outside it.

The paradox is that the deeper the cut, the more real the freedom. People who make small gestures — who fantasize about leaving but never step out — may feel momentary relief, but the cage remains intact. It is the bold cuts, the ones that rupture identity, that bring true escape. To walk away from wealth, to end a long marriage, to leave a community, to abandon a lifelong profession — these cuts bleed, but they also cleanse. They strip you of camouflage and leave you bare. And bare is where freedom begins.

I knew a woman who left her role as CEO of a major company to work with refugees. She told me she cried in hotel rooms for months, grieving the loss of status, income, and identity. Yet she said those tears were necessary. "I was washing off the old life," she explained. "Every sob was a layer of armor I didn't need anymore." The cut bled for a long time, but the healing revealed a person she hadn't met before. She said she felt human again.

The first cut also recalibrates your sense of scale. Once you've paid with blood, smaller costs seem trivial. The person who left a marriage will find it easier to leave a toxic friendship. The person who quit a secure job will find it easier to say no to smaller obligations. The scar reminds you that you've survived worse. This is why people who escape once often escape again. The first wound builds resilience. You stop fearing loss the way you once did, because you know you can survive it.

But scars can also tempt nostalgia. People look back at their old cages with a strange fondness. They remember the comfort, the routines, the approval. They forget the suffocation. This is another danger of the first cut: memory softens the bars. People romanticize captivity after they've escaped it, especially when freedom feels hard. It is tempting to crawl back. But the scar will not let you. The body remembers pain even when the mind lies. And if you listen, the scar will whisper: don't go back.

Cultures treat scarred escapees with ambivalence. Some admire them, casting them as visionaries or rebels. Others resent them, branding them failures or traitors. Both reactions miss the point. The cut is not for spectators. It is for the escapee. The wound is not a performance but a necessity. Whether others applaud or condemn is irrelevant. The bars were cut, and that is what matters.

Escape always costs, but the cost is also a teacher. It shows you what you were willing to pay and what you weren't. It shows you what mattered more than safety. It shows you the limits of your endurance and the beginning of your freedom. People imagine they can calculate these costs in advance, but they can't. The price is always higher or lower than expected. Higher in the pain of loss. Lower in the exhilaration of surviving it. You only know once you've cut.

The deepest cuts change not only your life but your vision. You start to see cages everywhere. You recognize the language of excuses, the weight of obligations, the smell of fear. You become less tolerant of captivity, both in yourself and in others. This can be isolating, because you can no longer sit comfortably with people who have chosen to stay. But it is also liberating, because you now know what most deny: the cost of freedom is pain, and the cost of captivity is everything.

The first cut is remembered not only for its pain but for the way it rearranges everything that comes after. Once you've made it, the world never looks the same. You measure choices differently, weigh costs differently, and see cages differently. The wound becomes a reference point, a scar you carry into every decision. It whispers: you survived. It reminds you: you bled, but you lived. And that memory changes what you are willing to do next.

Many people fear this scar, as if it marks them as damaged. But scars are proof of survival. They are maps etched into the body that say: here was the place I chose freedom over safety. They are ugly to some, intimidating to others, but to the escapee, they are sacred. They are reminders that the cut was real, that freedom was not free, that life demanded a price, and you paid it. Without scars, you would forget. You would soften. The cage would begin to look tempting again. The scar prevents that. It is your private monument to courage.

I once met a man who left a monastery after twenty years. He described the loneliness that followed as unbearable, the guilt as suffocating, the shame as overwhelming. But when he rolled up his sleeve and showed me the tattoo he got after leaving, he smiled. "This is my scar," he said. "It reminds me I chose life." His body carried the wound of exile, but it also carried the proof of freedom. He told me the tattoo wasn't a decoration. It was an anchor. When doubts whispered that he had made a mistake, he looked at it and remembered: he had survived the cut.

The deepest lesson of the first cut is that you cannot serve two masters. You cannot cling to the cage and escape it at the same time. You cannot keep reputation and freedom, loyalty and honesty, security and truth. You must choose. And the choice will hurt. The wound is proof that you did not settle for compromise. You tore yourself free, however clumsily, however painfully, because compromise was another word for captivity.

This is why those who cut are often misunderstood. People ask why they couldn't stay a little longer, compromise a little more, ease the transition. But cages do not allow gentle exits. They rely on inertia, guilt, loyalty, and fear. If you wait until you can leave cleanly, you will never leave. The only way out is to cut, and cuts are never clean. They are jagged, bloody, raw. That is what makes them real.

The first cut also reveals something the cage never wanted you to know: you are stronger than you imagined. The bars were built to convince you that you could not survive without them. The marriage told you that you would collapse alone. The job told you that you would starve without the paycheck. The system told you that you would fail without its approval. But when you cut and survived, you proved them all liars. That knowledge cannot be taken from you. It becomes part of your marrow.

I think of a woman who left her family's farm, breaking a lineage that stretched back centuries. She was ostracized, cursed, and erased from family records. For years, she wandered, unsure of who she was without the land. But when I met her, she was radiant. "They said I would die without them," she told me. "But I didn't. I thrived." The wound had nearly killed her, but the survival had remade her. The scar was visible in her stories, her silences, her strength. She no longer feared any other cut. Once you've made the first, the others come easier.

And that is the strange gift of the first cut. It teaches you that pain is not the end but the beginning. It hurts, yes. It bleeds, yes. It leaves scars, yes. But it also liberates. It proves that the cage is not eternal, that the bars are not fatal, that you are not as fragile as you were taught to believe. Pain becomes teacher, scar becomes scripture, and freedom becomes habit.

The deepest cut is the one that changes your story. Before it, you were someone who stayed. After it, you are someone who left. That change ripples through everything. You walk differently, speak differently, and decide differently. You no longer ask if you can survive loss. You know you can. You no longer ask if freedom is possible. You know it is. The first cut is the deepest because it transforms not only your circumstances but your identity. You are no longer a prisoner who dreams. You are an escapee who acts.

Chapter 8: Pressure Points

Every system has weak spots. Every cage, no matter how solid, has a seam. The trick of survival thinking is that it teaches you to adapt to the strongest parts of the structure — the routines, the authority, the walls that look immovable. But escape thinking turns your eyes to the fractures. You stop asking, "How do I endure this?" and start asking, "Where is the point of pressure that makes the whole thing shake?"

This shift matters because most people imagine escape requires enormous strength. They believe they must stockpile courage, amass resources, and wait until they are strong enough to overpower the bars. But power is rarely distributed evenly. The tiniest shove in the right place can move things that brute force never could. The art of escape is the art of leverage.

I once knew a man who had been trapped in debt for years. He worked long hours, paid religiously, but the interest devoured everything. For decades, he had been told there was no way out but to keep grinding. One day, he discovered the concept of bankruptcy. It terrified him — the stigma, the judgment, the paperwork. But when he pressed on that single point of the system, his life changed. He wiped away decades of financial captivity in one move. It wasn't painless, but it proved something: the cage wasn't absolute. It had a hinge, and he had found it.

The same principle applies to relationships. A woman I knew spent years bending under the weight of a manipulative partner. She tried therapy, compromise, and endless patience. Nothing worked. Then one day, she refused to answer his calls. That single act of silence shifted the balance. The power he had enjoyed evaporated because it had always depended on her participation. It wasn't strength that freed her. It was a refusal. That was the pressure point, and she pressed it.

Pressure points are rarely obvious until you start testing them. Systems are designed to look seamless, like fortress walls without cracks. But if you lean, if you poke, if you press, you discover soft spots. The company that insists you're indispensable panics when you threaten to resign. The family that insists you can never leave grows silent when you start packing bags. The voice inside your head that insists you'll collapse if you quit your job quiets once you've been unemployed for a month and are still alive. Every test redraws the map. You discover that the bars were not steel but plywood painted silver.

There is a myth that escape is about grand gestures, burning bridges, shouting truth, and smashing locks. But the reality is quieter. Escape begins with pressure applied in the right places, often in secret, often in silence. You skip one meeting. You decline one invitation. You tell one forbidden truth. These acts look small from the outside, but they tilt the structure. Suddenly, the cage doesn't feel inevitable anymore. Suddenly, the possibility of collapse seems real. That possibility is enough to keep you moving.

Systems rely on people not pressing. They rely on compliance, on inertia, on the belief that nothing can change. The unspoken rule is: don't test the bars. That's why even minor defiance is punished so harshly. The point isn't the act itself —

leaving work early, refusing a demand, questioning a rule. The point is the precedent. If you learn that one act of disobedience didn't kill you, you might try another. And then another. Soon, the cage shakes.

I once read about prisoners of war who discovered that simply tapping messages through walls to each other gave them strength. It was a small thing, invisible to guards, but it reminded them they weren't alone. The guards could control their food, their light, their sleep, but not the rhythm of taps. That rhythm became a lifeline. It was leverage. The tiniest act of resistance reminded them they still had power. That is the essence of a pressure point: something small that shifts the entire equation.

Finding pressure points requires attentiveness. You must notice what the system needs from you, then ask: What happens if I withdraw it? Employers need your labor. Families need your obedience. Friends need your compliance. Creditors need your payments. The cage always takes more than it gives. So the question becomes: what if I stop feeding it? Even slightly, even temporarily. What happens when I deprive it of what it assumes it will always receive?

Not every push works. Some bars are reinforced. Some refusals bring punishment. But each test teaches you something. You learn where the cage is strong and where it is weak. You learn that you don't have to overpower the whole system to escape. You only have to find the hinge. Press enough times in the right place, and the door swings open.

The discovery of a pressure point is like a revelation. It changes how you see everything around you. What looked like solid walls now look like a collection of joints, seams, and hinges. You realize the cage is not a monolith but an assembly of moving parts, all of which depend on your cooperation to function. And once you see that, the whole structure seems less intimidating.

I remember speaking with a teacher who worked under a brutal administration. Micromanaged, underpaid, and blamed for every failure, she believed she had no choice but to endure. Then one day, she refused to take on an unpaid duty that had been piled onto her workload. She braced for punishment, expecting reprimands or dismissal. Instead, nothing happened. Her refusal was met with silence. For the first time, she realized her captors' power was partly bluff. They had relied on her obedience, not on actual enforcement. That refusal became her compass. From then on, she pressed more. The cage had looked absolute. Now she saw it was brittle.

Pressure points matter because they reveal something survival thinking never admits: cages are fragile. They look permanent because everyone agrees to pretend they are. But the moment someone pushes, the performance falters. The boss who seemed unshakeable scrambles when talent threatens to leave. The partner who seemed controlling shrinks when you stop apologizing. The creditor who seemed unstoppable suddenly offers "options" when you hint at default. These moments don't destroy the cage outright, but they prove it isn't indestructible. And that proof is fuel.

The most powerful pressure points are often internal. Habits of thought, assumptions of weakness, beliefs about inevitability. I knew a man who always said he could never live outside the city. He was certain he needed the noise, the speed, the anonymity. Then he was forced by circumstance to spend six months in a rural town. To his surprise, he thrived. The silence he feared gave him peace. The absence of distraction gave him focus. His old belief collapsed, and with it collapsed years of excuses. The cage had never been real. It was a thought he had mistaken for truth. The pressure point wasn't a system. It was his own assumption.

This is why experimentation is vital. You cannot always predict which pressure points will yield. You have to test them. Try saying no to a minor obligation. Try ignoring one demand. Try withdrawing one ounce of energy from the system. Sometimes nothing happens. Sometimes you feel punishment. But sometimes the whole edifice wobbles. And once it wobbles, you realize it can fall.

Cultures discourage this testing because it exposes their fragility. That is why people who question authority are ridiculed or silenced. Not because their questions are dangerous on their own, but because they encourage others to start pressing too. One refusal leads to another, one "why" echoes into a chorus. The cage is most vulnerable not when it is attacked from outside, but when those inside start doubting it. Doubt is the finger on the hinge.

I think of a woman who grew up in a strict religious community. She followed every rule, attended every service, lived every tradition. But one day, she skipped a single gathering. Nothing catastrophic happened. No punishment, no divine wrath, absence. That small act of disobedience grew into a habit. Soon she realized the whole system relied on her presence, her compliance, her silence. Without them, it was weaker than she had imagined. That was her first taste of leverage. She had pressed a pressure point, and the cage had flinched.

The mistake most people make is believing they need to attack the whole cage at once. They imagine escape as heroic, dramatic, all or nothing. But cages don't fall that way. They crumble under accumulated pressure. Each push, each refusal, each test is a chisel tap. The wall resists, then resists, then suddenly cracks. The collapse looks sudden from the outside, but from the inside, you know it was years of quiet pressure.

What makes pressure points so powerful is that they turn captivity into a negotiation. Instead of accepting terms dictated by others, you begin to alter the terms. You shift the balance of power one act at a time. You prove to yourself and to the system that you are not entirely compliant. And that shift in posture matters more than the act itself. Once you see yourself as someone who can press, you stop being someone who only endures.

The secret is not to look for perfection. Not every push will succeed. Some doors will stay locked; some walls won't budge. But the act of pressing changes you. It turns you from passive to active, from victim to agent. Even failure teaches you where the strength of the system lies. And that knowledge is itself leverage. You now know where not to waste your energy, and where to double it.

The cage depends on your belief in its permanence. Pressure points prove otherwise. Each time you find one, you chip away at inevitability. Each time you press, you remind yourself that you are not powerless. And once you've tasted that reminder, once you've felt the wobble of the walls, you cannot go back to the silence of endurance. The system no longer looks absolute. It looks negotiable. And negotiation is the first step to escape.

The more you practice pressing against the bars, the more you realize that cages are not only personal but systemic. They aren't jobs, relationships, or debts. They are entire networks of expectation and control. And the same principle applies at this larger scale: systems have pressure points too.

Think of governments that collapse not under foreign invasion but under a single spark of protest. One marcher, one act of defiance, one refusal that spreads like fire. What begins as one person's private act becomes collective leverage. The system doesn't fall because it was overwhelmed by force. It falls because its weakest seam was pressed long enough for others to see it.

History is filled with these moments. A woman refuses to sit at the back of a bus. A worker walks off a factory line. A student throws a question into the silence of a lecture hall. These acts look small in isolation, but they reveal vulnerabilities that the system worked hard to conceal. Once the pressure point is exposed, others press too. The cage that looked immovable buckles under its own weight.

The same is true in smaller contexts. A family that has operated under unspoken rules for generations suddenly falters when one member refuses to play along. A community that enforces conformity begins to fracture when one person leaves and thrives outside. A workplace obsessed with overwork loses its spell when a single employee quits and lands somewhere better. These are not cracks in marble. They are cracks in plaster painted to look like stone. Once exposed, everyone sees how fragile the walls are.

But pressure points do not always require public defiance. Sometimes they are exploited in silence. A man stuck in an exploitative job quietly applies elsewhere, and the moment he gets an offer, the company scrambles to retain him. A woman in a rigid household begins saving money in secret, building the option of departure long before announcing it. A student overwhelmed by loans discovers one loophole in the system and uses it to unshackle decades of debt. None of these moves is dramatic. But each is decisive. Each exploits a pressure point the cage did not expect them to see.

What matters is not how loud the act is but how true it feels. When you press in the right place, you feel the tremor. You sense the weakness. The cage that once seemed like iron feels suddenly hollow. That tremor is addictive because it proves the impossible is not impossible after all.

And once you know this, you cannot help but see leverage everywhere. You start noticing where systems overreach, where people bluff, where rules are arbitrary. You realize how much of captivity depends on fear rather than fact. The boss who insists "we don't have a budget" but suddenly finds it when you threaten to leave. The parent who insists, "You'll never survive without us," but grows silent when you prove otherwise. The creditor who insists "there's no alternative" but offers three once you refuse. Pressure points turn absolutes into negotiations.

I knew a man who thought his landlord held absolute power. Rent increases, endless restrictions, constant surveillance. He felt trapped until one day he simply moved out. The landlord panicked. Vacancies meant vulnerability. Suddenly, the man realized the cage had always been mutual: he had been trapped by fear, but the landlord had been dependent on his compliance. The pressure point wasn't confrontation. It was a departure.

This is the nature of pressure: it doesn't weaken the bars. It reveals how much the bars depended on you. The cage is not as one-sided as it pretends to be. It needs your labor, your money, your silence, your loyalty. Without those, it shakes. And that knowledge is dangerous, because once you see it, you stop treating the system as invincible. You start treating it as negotiable, manipulable, fragile.

The danger, of course, is overconfidence. Not every wall will collapse at the first push. Some cages punish pressing severely. Systems are not infinitely pliable, and misjudging their strength can hurt. But even failed attempts teach you something. They map the architecture of control. They show you where not to waste energy. And they remind you that the real danger lies not in pressing, but in never pressing at all.

The greatest gift of finding pressure points is not the collapse of one specific cage but the shift in identity it creates. You stop seeing yourself as powerless. You stop believing that your only role is to endure. You start seeing yourself as someone who can act, someone who can change the equation. That shift ripples into everything. Once you press one bar, you are never the same again.

The real revelation of pressure points is that they redefine power. You begin to see that the cage was never external; it was built from your own compliance. Every rule you obeyed without question, every fear you never tested, every compromise you convinced yourself was maturity — all of it reinforced the walls. When you press, you are not only testing the system. You are testing yourself. You are asking: Do I believe the story I've been told about my own limits?

I knew a man who thought he could never live without the approval of his parents. For decades, he lived in their shadow, shaping every choice to keep their pride intact. Then one day, exhausted, he refused to explain himself. He made a decision and didn't ask permission. The reaction was explosive — anger, guilt, silence. But then something strange happened: he realized he was still breathing. The catastrophe he had imagined never came. The cage was mostly inside his head, and pressing against it dissolved decades of imagined steel into vapor.

This is why pressure points are terrifying: they expose the lies you've believed. You tell yourself you couldn't survive without this job, this marriage, this approval. You press, and suddenly you see you can. That moment is destabilizing, even disorienting. Freedom is not about breaking systems but about breaking illusions. And illusions die hard.

But once an illusion dies, you are never the same. You cannot go back to believing the cage was unbreakable. You carry with you the memory of its tremor, the knowledge of its fragility. And that knowledge spreads. The next time you face a new cage, you are quicker to spot the seam, bolder to press the hinge. Escape becomes less a miracle and more a method.

The secret that cages don't want you to know is that they cannot withstand sustained pressure. They may resist at first. They may punish you. They may even close ranks. But no system can survive once enough people stop feeding it. Every regime, every corporation, every toxic family dynamic relies on a steady diet of silence and obedience. When silence cracks, when obedience falters, the whole thing shakes. That is why even small acts of refusal are treated as threats. They are not dangerous in themselves. They are dangerous because they might spread.

I once spoke with a man who left a cult-like organization after twenty years. He told me what finally broke him was not a dramatic confrontation but a question whispered by a friend: "What if they're wrong?" That question became unbearable. He couldn't stop pressing it in his head. Eventually, he left, and when he did, others followed. Not because he begged them to, but because his departure showed that departure was possible. His act of pressing revealed the pressure point. The cage had always depended on belief. Once that belief cracked, others could see daylight too.

The most important lesson of pressure points is not how to break free but how to live free. You don't wait for cages to form around you and then hope you'll be strong enough to smash them. You live with the habit of pressing. You cultivate the reflex of asking: Where is the seam? You treat every demand, every expectation, every structure with skepticism until it proves itself worthy of your compliance. That posture does not make you cynical. It makes you vulnerable to captivity.

Because captivity thrives on unconsciousness. It thrives on people who never test, never press, never question. Escape thrives on the opposite. It thrives on people who notice, who experiment, who refuse to surrender their agency without proof. Pressure points are not tools for escape. They are tools for life outside the cage.

The cage will always insist you are powerless. Pressure points whisper otherwise. They remind you that every wall, no matter how solid, hides a seam. They remind you that the strongest-looking locks depend on your cooperation. They remind you that even the smallest act of defiance can ripple through the structure. To live with this knowledge is to live with leverage. And leverage, once discovered, never leaves you.

Chapter 9: Burn the Map

Every escape demands a map, or so we're told. We are raised to believe that life is navigable: milestones marked out, routes drawn, destinations fixed. School, career, marriage, mortgage, retirement. Even rebellion is mapped — "gap years," career pivots, midlife crises, all packaged like alternate routes on the same chart. The message is simple: stay on the map. It has been drawn for you. It is safe.

But the cruel trick of maps is that they are written by people who benefit from your obedience. The map of success was drawn by employers who need compliant workers. The map of family duty was drawn by parents who need loyalty to define their worth. The map of consumption was drawn by industries that profit when you mistake buying for living. None of these maps was made with your freedom in mind. They were made to keep you moving in predictable loops.

Escape means throwing those maps into the fire. Not adding them, not redrawing them, not choosing a different route — burning them. Because the moment you follow a path laid out by someone else, you are back in a cage. The walls may be wider, the scenery prettier, but the logic is the same: you are not choosing, you are following.

I once knew a man who worked for decades as an engineer, saving diligently, waiting for retirement to finally live. When he reached sixty-five, the market collapsed, his pension evaporated, and his health faltered. The map had betrayed him. "I did everything right," he told me bitterly, "and it led nowhere." The map hadn't been a guarantee. It had been a leash, keeping him docile while others reaped the rewards of his labor. Burning the map would have meant asking, years earlier, what he wanted instead of what he was told to want.

Burning the map is terrifying because it means stepping into uncertainty. The map promises clarity, direction, and milestones. Without it, you are left with a blank page. People crave certainty so much that they cling to bad maps rather than face emptiness. They would rather walk paths that lead nowhere than admit they don't know where to go. But the blank page is not emptiness. It is a possibility. And possibility is the soil of freedom.

I knew a woman who abandoned her career in law after realizing she had pursued it only to meet expectations. When she left, everyone asked, "What's next?" She admitted she didn't know. The admission shocked them. It even shocked her. But she refused to replace one map with another. Instead, she wandered, tried new things, lived without a plan. The uncertainty was brutal at first. But slowly, she began to build a life shaped by curiosity instead of obligation. She told me later, "Not knowing became my freedom."

The map is seductive because it offers legitimacy. When you follow it, no one questions you. You are praised for staying the course, admired for stability, and envied for predictability. But that praise is counterfeit. It is the system rewarding you for captivity. Burn the map, and the praise turns to judgment. People call you lost, irresponsible, reckless. They pity you. They mock you. They whisper about failure. But what they are expressing is fear — fear that if your wandering leads somewhere true, their obedience will look like folly.

The truth is that every meaningful escape requires abandoning the map. There is no drawn line to freedom. There is only wilderness. And wilderness is where you find out who you are when you are not following instructions. It is where you learn to build, to adapt, to choose without guidance. It is where you stop being a passenger and start being an author.

But make no mistake: wilderness is hard. It is lonely, disorienting, and frightening. You will doubt yourself constantly. You will long for the comfort of the old map, the certainty of knowing what comes next. That longing is natural. But if you resist it, if you keep walking, something shifts. The blank page begins to fill, not with someone else's lines, but with your own. And those lines, messy and uncertain though they may be, are the first true marks of freedom.

The first days without a map are the loudest. Everyone has an opinion about your direction. They ask for timelines, deliverables, and proof that this isn't a drift with better branding. They want a plan written in bullet points so they can stop worrying about you. They want a narrative that resembles the old one: where are you in five years, what's the ladder, what's the endgame. The demand is seductive because it offers relief. Give them a plan and they'll give you peace. But the price of that peace is the return to a cage. The moment you script your next year to soothe other people's anxiety, you've handed your compass to the crowd.

Maps are for moving through landscapes that don't change. Wilderness changes. It shifts beneath your feet. The river you intended to ford becomes a flood by morning. The clearing you planned to sleep in turns swamps by night. This is why people cling to maps even when they fail. If the world is dynamic, the map is always wrong, but at least it is comforting. Burning the map is not an act of contempt for planning; it's an act of humility in the face of uncertainty. You admit the world is too alive to be domesticated by a single route.

So how do you move without one? You trade routes for instruments. Pilots fly through clouds by instruments, not by landmarks. Sailors navigate by stars, currents, and wind, not a dotted line sketched by someone at a desk. Wilderness travel is done by feel, attention, and iteration. In life, the instruments are principles and constraints. You keep a handful of non-negotiables, and you let everything else flex. Never trade your health for money. Never stay where you cannot tell the truth. Never bind your identity to a title. Never sign a contract that requires your silence. Instruments, not itinerary.

I knew a chef who torched his plan mid-career. He had mapped it perfectly: culinary school, apprenticeship, sous-chef, head chef by forty, his own place by forty-five. It was immaculate and dead. He noticed that he had become an administrator of a kitchen he didn't care about. The map promised progress and delivered repetition. He burned it and went back to the line, then left the line to cook private dinners, then abandoned the city for a small town where he cooked three nights a week and fished the other four. There was no elevator pitch. When people demanded a plan, he gave them a principle: "I only cook what I can source within a day's drive." That was his instrument. Everything else changed with the weather.

When you burn the map, you also burn the tyranny of credentials. Maps love credentials because they keep traffic orderly. Get the degree, collect the stamp, and wait at the light until it turns green. But wayfinding doesn't require permission. It requires competence and curiosity. I've watched people spend years acquiring certificates to qualify for work they could learn in six months by doing it badly until they learned how to do it well. The map tells them to queue. The wilderness says: start, then get better. The credential is often a toll on a road you don't need to drive.

Of course, wandering is not the point. You can get lost in the name of freedom as easily as you can get trapped in the name of safety. The difference between wandering and wayfinding is feedback. Wayfinding is structured improvisation: act, observe, and. You set an intention, move a short distance, check reality, and correct. You run time-boxed experiments instead of making life-long vows. Ninety days without alcohol. Six months living on half your previous income. A year away from the industry you swore was your destiny. The horizon stays open, but the steps are concrete. You are not drifting. You are testing.

This is where most people fail without a map: they confuse uncertainty with aimlessness. They believe if they can't explain exactly where they're going, they must not be going anywhere. But you can measure direction without predicting destination. You can ask simpler, harder questions: Is my energy higher after this work than before it? Did I need to lie to get through today? Do I feel smaller after an hour with these people, or larger? Those answers are your northings and eastings. Chart them and they'll draw a line more honest than any roadmap.

Burning the map also exposes how much of "strategy" is imitation with better copywriting. People borrow other people's paths, repaint them, then suffer when the terrain doesn't match the brochure. The founder who tries to copy a unicorn playbook in a different market. The artist who imitates a mentor's career without their temperament. The couple who buys a house because it seemed adult, then discovers homeownership was someone else's dream. Imitation is efficient and deadly. The map's routes look smart because they are well-traveled. You forget they were built for feet that aren't yours.

The cost of burning the map is that you will often look foolish. You will arrive at dead ends. You will misread the weather. Your friends will collect your stumbles and offer them back as evidence that you should have stayed on the road. But failure looks different off-map. On the map, failure is a detour back to the highway. Off the map, failure is data. It tells you where not to go again. The person who treats failures as data becomes untouchable. They don't waste time defending identity. They treat identity like a hypothesis. When it breaks, they ad.

There is a quiet discipline to life without a map: quitting as a skill. Not dramatic quitting. Clean quitting. The kind where you stop early when the signal says stop, before sunk costs turn into cement. The map tells you that perseverance is always good. The wilderness tells you perseverance is good only if the direction is still true. Quitting on time preserves the fuel you'll need for what matters. Every cage is filled with people who stayed because the map said "keep going." They confused endurance with wisdom. Burn the map, and you learn to exit cleanly.

When you live this way, the world starts to open in strange places. Possibilities appear where the map insisted there were none. A conversation in a laundromat becomes a collaboration. A side project pays your rent. A friendship becomes a working partnership. The map would have screened these as noise; your instruments read them as signals. Without pre-approved routes, you notice trails that were invisible to the obedient. The landscape becomes legible again, not because it is simple but because you are finally paying attention.

People will ask you, eventually, for the new map. They will want you to bottle your wayfinding. They'll ask for a course, a system, a checklist. They will beg you to draw lines they can follow. Resist the temptation to become the cartographer of your own freedom. The moment you convert wayfinding into a fixed route for others, you forget the first law of wilderness: what worked once will not necessarily work again. Share principles, share instruments, share errors. Do not draw them a road. Teach them to look up at the sky and read.

The irony is that as you keep moving this way, you will accumulate a kind of internal atlas, not of roads but of patterns. You'll learn which negotiations always turn toxic, no matter the pay. You'll learn which kinds of collaborators are oxygen and which are carbon monoxide. You'll learn which geographies wake you up and which shut you down. This atlas is personal. It can't be gifted. It has to be earned by walking.

The point of burning the map isn't to prove that maps are evil. It's to refuse the superstition that your life can be reduced to one. Routes will sometimes appear. Seasons will sometimes require plans. Use them, then toss them when the weather changes. A plan is a tool, not a god. The second you bow to it, you're back in a chapel built by someone else.

In the end, the wilderness teaches a simple hierarchy: compass over map, principles over plans, experiments over forecasts, honesty over approval. If a line on paper asks you to betray those, set it on fire. Watch the ash drift. Feel the heat on your hands. Then take a step, small and true, and another after that. The ground will tell you if you're moving right. The sky will tell you if you're still you. And if you listen long enough, you'll realize you weren't lost. You were finally off the road.

Once you've burned the map, you start noticing how much of your old life was spent performing certainty. You answered questions you didn't believe in, plotted futures you didn't want, nodded along to plans that felt like costumes. Without the map, the performance collapses. You no longer have easy answers to the questions people love to ask: What's next? Where do you see yourself? How will you know you've succeeded? The honest answer is unsettling: you don't know. At first, it feels like shame. Later, it feels like honesty. Eventually, it feels like freedom.

But this honesty comes at a cost. To admit you don't know where you're going is to reject the currency of credibility. Maps make you legible to others. They reassure people that you're normal, predictable, and safe. Without one, you become illegible. Employers hesitate. Families worry. Friends distance themselves. You are no longer playing a role they understand. You are an unmarked figure walking across blank paper. And that is terrifying to people who rely on maps to orient themselves.

Illegibility, however, is also power. When you cannot be read by their maps, you cannot be controlled by them. A boss can threaten promotion and punishment, but if you don't measure your life by their ladder, the threat dissolves. A family can guilt you about milestones, but if you don't see life as a series of milestones, the guilt loses its teeth. Legibility is captivity. Illegibility is freedom. The less predictable you are to their maps, the harder it is for them to trap you.

This illegibility bleeds into identity. On the map, identity is a cluster of labels: student, spouse, manager, homeowner. Off the map, identity becomes fluid, shifting, experimental. You stop answering the question "Who are you?" with nouns and start answering it with verbs. Not "I am a teacher," but "I teach." Not "I am a writer," but "I write." Not "I am an entrepreneur," but "I build." Verbs are harder to trap than nouns. Verbs keep moving. The moment you define yourself by action rather than role, the cage struggles to keep up.

I knew a man who clung desperately to his title as "doctor." It was his anchor, his legitimacy, his worth. When he left medicine, he nearly collapsed. Without the noun, he felt naked. It took years for him to realize he hadn't lost his identity — he had lost the cage. He was still healed. He still taught. He still guided. Those verbs were alive. The noun had been the prison. Burning the map freed him to see that his essence was not the credential but the action.

Burning the map also redefines success. On the map, success is always deferred: the next promotion, the next house, the next accolade. Off the map, success collapses into the present. Success becomes answering: Did today align with my principles? Did I act in integrity? Did I create something real? Did I move toward life instead of away from it? These measures are harder to parade, harder to monetize, harder to brag about at reunions. But they are also harder to fake. They are lived in the body, not printed on paper.

This shift terrifies people who are addicted to external validation. They will accuse you of settling, of wasting potential, of being unambitious. What they mean is: you are no longer competing on the map they worship. You have stepped into a different game; one they cannot measure. That illegibility makes them nervous. They try to drag you back by redefining your choices as failure. Resist this. Remember that maps are judgment machines. Without one, their judgment has no coordinates.

Another gift of burning the map is resilience. When the mapped life collapses — when markets crash, when institutions fail, when industries evaporate — those still on the map panic. Their path has vanished, and they have no compass. But if you've lived without one, collapse feels familiar. You've trained in uncertainty. You know how to wayfind. You know how to improvise, to iterate, to move without guarantees. To the mapped, collapse is death. To the unmapped, collapse is Tuesday.

I once knew a woman whose company went bankrupt overnight. Colleagues were shattered, unable to imagine life outside the structure they had trusted. She was frightened too, but she had been side-stepping maps for years, freelancing, experimenting, living lean. "It was like watching everyone else drown in shallow water," she told me. "I knew how to swim without the pool." Burning the map hadn't freed her. It had trained her.

The irony is that burning the map doesn't leave you with nothing. It leaves you with everything. Every path becomes open, every horizon reachable, every experiment possible. The map limited you to roads already paved. The blank page gives you fields, forests, mountains, and oceans. Most of them will be hard. Some will be fatal. But they are yours to choose. And in choosing, you reclaim what the map stole: authorship of your own life.

The greatest fear of living without a map is that you will get lost forever. People cling to plans, milestones, and scripts because they believe wandering means ruin. But ruin only comes when you keep walking the wrong road because the map insists it leads somewhere. The wilderness has no such illusions. If you go the wrong way, reality corrects you. The weather turns. The terrain shifts. The signals are clear. You stop and turn. What looked like aimlessness becomes responsiveness. What looked like foolishness becomes resilience.

The irony is that burning the map doesn't eliminate guidance. It sharpens it. You start noticing signals you once ignored. The conversations that leave you alive versus the ones that leave you hollow. The projects that drain versus the ones that energize. The principles that endure versus the ones that crumble under pressure. These are not landmarks etched on paper; they are signs inscribed in your own body. And they are truer than any dotted line.

This way of living terrifies the mapped world because it resists control. You cannot be bribed with promotions if promotions don't define you. You cannot be threatened with exclusion if belonging is no longer your compass. You cannot be sold new coordinates if you have stopped believing in fixed destinations. To those still living on maps, you look reckless. To yourself, you look alive.

I knew a man who used to say he felt "untethered" after quitting the corporate ladder. At first, there was panic. But over time, he realized the tether had never been safe. It had been a leash. Untethered, he was not drifting. He was free. "I thought I needed a map," he told me, "but all I needed was a horizon." That shift of perspective is what burning the map makes possible: you stop measuring by routes and start measuring by direction.

The point is not to prove you are better without a plan. The point is to refuse captivity disguised as planning. Maps are useful for travel across conquered terrain. They are lethal when applied to living. Life is not conquered terrain. It is wilderness, alive and shifting, and it requires attention, honesty, and courage more than it requires instructions.

When you burn the map, you are not promising never to stumble. You are promising never to walk blindly again. You are promising that if you fall, it will be in pursuit of your own horizon, not in obedience to someone else's line. You are promising that your life will be authored, not administered. That promise is the essence of escape.

Chapter 10: The High Price of Freedom

Every escape leaves a bill on the table. You can walk out of a cage, but you don't walk out without paying. The currency varies—money, reputation, relationships, even identity—but the charge is inevitable. People who fantasize about freedom often imagine it as clean: the door swings open, they step into the sun, the credits roll. But life isn't cinema. The door swings open, and you discover that leaving costs more than staying ever did.

This is why most people refuse to escape even when they know they should. It isn't ignorance of the cage. It's the dread of the price. The bars look heavy, but the receipt is heavier. You will pay in lost approval. You will pay in uncertainty. You will pay in loneliness. You will pay in fear. The question is not whether freedom is expensive. It is whether captivity is worth the hidden interest it charges.

I once spoke with a woman who walked out of a marriage after twenty-five years. She had been suffocating for most of them, silenced by duty and fear of judgment. The cut was brutal. She lost her house, her community, and her financial stability. She told me that for two years, she wondered daily if she had made a mistake. But then her eyes lit up. "I started breathing again," she said. "For the first time in decades, I knew who I was without him." The cost was steep, but the bill for staying would have been steeper: a life unlived.

Freedom extracts payment up front. Captivity extracts it slowly, in installments; you barely notice until the debt is unpayable. That's the trick: the cage hides the bill in routines and compromises, while freedom slaps it on the table in one blow. You feel the pain immediately. You bleed all at once. But that pain is finite. Captivity's price is infinite. It charges in regret, in resentment, in years you never get back.

The high price of freedom is often social. You will be judged, mocked, and pitied. People will whisper that you are reckless, selfish, unstable. The criticism cuts because it comes from people you once leaned on. But their condemnation is also proof you've left their cage. They need you to stay because your escape threatens their story. When you leave, they feel the walls of their own prisons. So they punish you for reminding them. Their anger is not about your freedom. It is about their fear.

I knew a man who abandoned a lucrative law career to pursue music. His peers called him irresponsible. His family treated him like a dropout. He lived in a dingy apartment, scraping together gigs, humiliated by the contrast between his past prestige and his present struggle. But when I asked if he regretted it, he shook his head. "Every insult hurt," he said, "but none of them hurt as much as staying." The insults faded. The music didn't. That was the transaction: pride traded for truth.

Financial cost is the one people fear most. To walk away from a steady paycheck, to sell possessions, to downsize, to lose status symbols—these feel like death in a culture that equates money with life. And the fear isn't unfounded. Poverty is a cage of its own. But sometimes the real poverty is spiritual: years spent rich in salary but bankrupt in purpose. The price of freedom in dollars may be high, but the price of captivity in spirit is higher.

Freedom also charges in uncertainty. The map is gone. The path is unwritten. You don't know what's next, and that void is terrifying. People crave predictability so much that they will choose misery with certainty over possibility without it. But uncertainty is not a flaw of freedom. It is the proof of it. The wilderness feels dangerous because it is alive. Captivity feels safe because it is dead. The price of freedom is learning to live with unpredictability instead of fearing it.

The loneliest bill freedom demands is connection. When you leave a cage, you leave behind the people who prefer to stay. Some drift away in silence. Others slam the door. Either way, you walk lighter but also lonelier. At least at first. The void aches. You miss the familiarity of voices, even if those voices silenced you. You miss the comfort of company, even if it was a company that chained you. Loneliness is the tax freedom extracted before new connections form.

But those who pay discover something extraordinary: the people who arrive after the escape are different. They aren't tied to you by expectation or duty. They are drawn to you as you are, not as you pretend to be. The relationships are fewer, but they are sharper, truer, and less fragile. You realize that the cost of losing the old was simply the price of making room for the new.

The high price of freedom is not something to be minimized or romanticized. It is something to be faced directly. Escape is costly, but captivity is lethal. You will lose money, reputation, approval, and stability. But you will gain something the cage could never sell you at any price: yourself.

The hidden price of freedom is doubt. No one warns you how relentless it is. The cage, for all its suffocation, was predictable. It had rules, however cruel. You knew your place, your role, your boundaries. Outside, there are no walls. At first, that feels exhilarating. Then it feels terrifying. You wake up at three in the morning, wondering if you've ruined your life. You second-guess every decision. You wonder if the cage was so bad, if you made the wound deeper than necessary, and if you should crawl back and apologize. Doubt is the echo of captivity. The bars remain in your head long after you've left them behind.

I knew a woman who left a powerful religious community. At first, she was euphoric. She described it as "finally breathing after years underwater." But months later, she was paralyzed by guilt and uncertainty. Without the church to tell her what was right, she didn't know how to move. She doubted herself constantly, feared she had made a catastrophic mistake. Only after years of practice did she learn to trust her own instincts again. Freedom had cost her certainty, and rebuilding trust in herself was the most grueling payment she ever made.

Another high price of freedom is invisibility. Inside the cage, you were visible. People knew your name, your role, your function. You belonged to a narrative larger than yourself. Outside, you are no one's employee, no one's spouse, no one's subject. You become invisible, and invisibility can feel like annihilation. This is why many people crawl back to captivity: not because they love it, but because at least there they are seen. Freedom demands you rebuild visibility from the inside out. You must decide that being unseen is not the same as being nonexistent.

Then there is the physical cost. Escapes are exhausting. They drain the body as well as the mind. You sleep poorly, your nerves hum, your appetite disappears or swells. Stress rides your shoulders like lead. Captivity has its own health costs, but at least they accumulate slowly. Freedom bills you immediately. The body wobbles under the weight of change. Some people break down entirely. They collapse not because freedom is a mistake but because they underestimated how much energy it takes to rebuild from scratch.

The rebuilding is another cost rarely discussed. To walk out of a job, a marriage, or a belief system is only the beginning. What follows is reconstruction. You have to assemble a life without the scaffolding you once leaned on. That means finding new ways to earn, new ways to connect, new ways to define yourself. The cage may have been cruel, but it provided structure. Freedom demolishes structure and demands you build your own. That construction project is hard, lonely, and expensive. But it is also the only way to own your life.

And there is another price, the most unsettling of all: responsibility. Captivity allows you to outsource responsibility. You blame the boss, the spouse, the institution, the tradition. Freedom leaves no one to blame but yourself. If you fail, it is your failure. If you falter, it is your falter. This terrifies people because responsibility is heavy. But it is also the essence of escape. The price of freedom is that you must carry yourself entirely. And though it is daunting, it is also clarifying. You stop wasting time rehearsing excuses. You know every step forward is yours alone.

I once knew a man who quit his corporate career to start a business. It failed within a year. He was humiliated. People pointed to him as an example of reckless arrogance. But when I asked if he regretted it, he said no. "At least it was my failure," he told me. "I can live with that. What I couldn't live with was succeeding in something I hated." The failure was a bill he could pay. The alternative would have been a debt too large to bear.

The high price of freedom is cumulative. It charges in doubt, invisibility, exhaustion, rebuilding, and responsibility. Each one adds weight. Each one tempts you to crawl back into the cage. But the trick is to see these costs not as signs of mistake, but as evidence of freedom's reality. If freedom cost nothing, it would be worthless. If freedom didn't wound you, it wouldn't change you. The bill hurts precisely because the product is real.

This is the great misunderstanding of escape: people imagine the cut is the end. In truth, it is the beginning of the payment plan. You walk out wounded, trembling, doubting, invisible, exhausted. You pay every day for months or years. But slowly, the payments buy something priceless: self-respect, authenticity, clarity, truth. The debt shrinks, the scars toughen, the fear fades. And one day, you wake up and realize you are free not only in body but in mind. The price has been paid.

The deepest price of freedom is time. Not the years lost inside the cage—though those weigh heavily—but the years spent learning how to walk outside it. You don't step into freedom fully formed. You stagger. You limp. You learn balance the way a child does, one fall at a time. And this learning curve is brutal. You will waste energy. You will waste money. You will waste years chasing things that don't fit. This waste is not a failure. It is tuition. It is the cost of becoming fluent in a language you were never taught: the language of your own life.

I once met a man who left corporate law in his forties. He told me the first decade outside felt like chaos. He bounced between startups, creative projects, and even odd jobs. He was humiliated often, broke often, and confused constantly. But then he paused. "I paid ten years for the right to wake up without dread," he said. "I'd pay ten more if I had to." The time looked wasted to his peers. To him, it was the price of freedom, and he considered it a bargain.

The price also comes in reputation. Once you leave the map, people rarely update their opinion of you. You remain frozen in their eyes: the quitter, the divorcee, the dropout, the rebel. No matter how far you go, they will drag your old label behind you like a chain. This can feel suffocating, but in time, it becomes clarifying. You realize reputation is a prison you no longer live in. Their judgment says more about them than it does about you. Your life, not their memory of it, is the truth. The scar reminds you: you already paid for their condemnation. You don't need to buy it again.

The price shows up in the body too. Stress leaves scars beneath the skin. Years of tension, years of compromise, years of swallowing truth—these etch themselves into posture, breath, health. Escape doesn't erase them. In fact, the first years outside often intensify them. Sleepless nights, anxiety attacks, health scares. But over time, something shifts. The body recalibrates. Breath deepens. Shoulders unclench. The health that was leaking away inside the cage begins to return. This too is part of the payment plan: enduring the body's breakdown long enough to allow its recovery.

Another bill comes due in relationships. Freedom changes how you connect, sometimes painfully. You outgrow old friends, lose the patience for shallow bonds, and find yourself intolerant of games you once played easily. The loneliness deepens before it heals. But when new relationships form, they form on different ground. Shared cages no longer define your connections. Shared values, shared curiosity, shared courage take their place. You lose numbers but gain depth. The loss is the cost. The depth is the dividend.

Freedom also charges you with uncertainty that never entirely disappears. Even after years, even after successes, there are nights when you wonder if you ruined everything. The cage was cruel, but it was stable. Freedom is alive, and aliveness is unpredictable. You learn to live with doubt as background noise, like static on an old radio. At first, it drives you mad. Then it becomes part of the music. You don't escape doubt. You learn to walk with it. That adamant is its own price, and its own gift.

I often think of the metaphor of scar tissue. Scar tissue isn't smooth. It isn't flexible. It doesn't look like the skin around it. It's tougher, less sensitive, sometimes even ugly. But it is also proof of survival. Freedom leaves scar tissue in your psyche. You become less naive, less trusting of institutions, less tolerant of false promises. That toughness can feel heavy. It can make you cynical if you let it. But it can also make you discerning. You stop mistaking cages for homes. You stop mistaking loyalty contracts. You stop mistaking maps for life. The scar tissue itches sometimes, but it also protects you.

The price of freedom is steep. It will take your money, your time, your certainty, your reputation, and your ease. But what it gives in return is not luxury. It is true. And truth, once tasted, is addictive. You cannot go back to lies. You cannot unknow the feel of real breath. You cannot unlearn the knowledge that captivity was never safety. That knowledge alone is worth every bill, every scar, every sleepless night.

The highest price of freedom is that it never stops charging you. People think once the wound heals, once the scars form, the ledger clears. It doesn't. Freedom is not a single bill but a subscription you renew daily. Every day you remain outside the cage, you are paying. You pay in vigilance, in discomfort, in the constant refusal to sell yourself back for a cheaper life. And that ongoing cost is what makes freedom so rare. Most people will pay once in a dramatic gesture. Few will keep paying in silence, day after day, choice after choice.

The temptation to return never fully vanishes. Captivity whispers like a lover. It promises ease, certainty, and protection. It offers you maps, applause, and stability. On hard nights, those offers glow like neon. You imagine crawling back, apologizing, resuming the script. And you know, deep down, the cage would take you back. It always does. That is part of its power. Freedom means refusing that offer, again and again. Every "no" is a payment. Every refusal keeps the door from closing behind you.

I once spoke to a man who left a powerful corporate role. Ten years later, he confessed that not a week passed without the thought of going back. He missed the money, the status, the smoothness of being legible again. But then he laughed and said, "I also know the moment I sit back at that desk, I'll stop breathing." His freedom cost him wealth, reputation, and comfort. But captivity would have cost him life. He kept paying the fee of doubt because it was cheaper than suffocation.

Another price is separation. Once you have paid for freedom, you can never truly rejoin the world of the obedient. You can visit, but you can't belong. Their conversations about promotions, mortgages, and milestones feel like a language you once spoke but forgot. You smile, you nod, you understand the words, but they no longer have power over you. This separation is bittersweet. You lose belonging. But you gain something larger: perspective. You can see the cage for what it is. You can see choices that others pretend don't exist. You can see the wilderness stretching where their map ends. That sight is expensive. But once you've seen it, you cannot unsee it.

The last and perhaps most brutal cost is responsibility for others. Freedom isolates you at first, but later it attracts the lost. People begin to ask you for guidance. They see you've left and survived. They wonder if they can too. This is its own weight. You cannot hand them freedom like a gift. You cannot pay their price for them. You can only show them the scar, tell them the truth: it hurts, it costs, it scars, and it is worth it. Carrying that truth is another bill. You become a mirror that terrifies and inspires. Some will hate you for it. Some will cling to you for it. Either way, you are paying.

The high price of freedom is not a flaw. It is the guarantee. Anything free is usually worthless. The very fact that freedom demands payment is what gives it weight. It forces you to decide, every day, whether you are willing to live awake. Captivity charges in sleep. Freedom charges in awareness. Captivity takes quietly. Freedom demands to be open. One is a slow death. The other is a costly life.

What freedom gives you in exchange is not comfort, not ease, not applause. It gives you yourself. It gives you mornings without dread, nights without suffocation, choices that belong to you alone. It gives you the ability to die without the bitter taste of regret. That is worth every bill, every scar, every lonely hour. The price is high. The alternative is higher. And in the end, the only question worth asking is this: are you willing to pay in pain now, or in regret forever?

ACT THREE

Chapter 11: Designing Anti-Traps

The trouble with escape is that unless you design differently, you walk out of one cage straight into another. People burn their maps, cut ties, pay their price — and then, hungry for stability, they stitch together the same bars they just tore down. A new job that repeats the old dynamic. A new relationship that mirrors the same control. A new set of rules that calcifies into another prison. Escape is meaningless without design. The real skill isn't only jailbreaking. It is architecture.

To live free, you have to build anti-traps. Not perfect lives immune to pain — that doesn't exist — but systems that resist capture, choices that bend toward clarity, structures that force you to keep moving instead of hardening around you. The irony is that most cages were designed, too. They didn't appear by accident. Institutions, markets, traditions, even families, engineered them carefully to hold people in place. If captivity was designed, freedom must be as well.

The first principle of anti-trap design is optionality. Captivity thrives on narrowing choices. The fewer exits, the tighter the bars. Anti-traps multiply exits. Financially, this means you avoid debt that ties you to a single paycheck. Emotionally, it means you refuse relationships where love is conditional on obedience. Professionally, it means you build skills that travel — portable, flexible, valuable in more than one context. Optionality is not about hoarding; it is about refusing to be locked into one path.

I once met a man who was brilliant at his craft but had only one client. The day that the client disappeared, so did his freedom. He wasn't untalented. He was under-designed. He had built his life as a single point of failure. Anti-traps would have meant two clients, five clients, ten. Freedom wasn't in brilliance; it was in redundancy.

The second principle is clarity of values. Most cages exploit fuzziness. They trap you by convincing you that survival is virtue, loyalty is love, and obedience is respect. If you don't know your values, you will live by someone else's. Anti-traps begin with a brutal audit: what do you refuse to trade? Health for money? Integrity for approval? Curiosity for comfort? Write it down. Repeat it until it burns into your spine. Cages collapse when values are clear because manipulation loses its grip.

The third principle is constraints by choice. People imagine freedom as boundless, but boundless choice is another trap. It overwhelms, paralyzes, and exhausts. Anti-traps mean setting the right constraints yourself instead of inheriting the wrong ones from others. The writer decides they will only work four hours a day. The worker who refuses jobs that demand dishonesty. The parent who will not raise children in silence. These constraints do not imprison. They guide. They hold space open for the things that matter.

Then there is the design for reversibility. Captivity often begins with irreversible decisions. Mortgages, marriages, and careers are locked in by sunk costs. Anti-traps preserve the ability to walk away. Rent instead of buy. Freelance instead of full-time. Experiment before committing. Keep contracts short. Avoid obligations that last longer than your conviction. If a choice cannot be reversed, it is not freedom — it is a potential cage waiting to snap.

I knew a woman who treated every new venture as a pilot. Three months, then evaluate. If it worked, she extended. If it didn't, she exited. People called her flaky. She called herself free. She had designed her life so no single decision could shackle her. The world saw instability. She lived in resilience.

The last principle is community without captivity. Humans need belonging, but belonging is the softest snare. Anti-traps mean finding or building circles where loyalty is voluntary, where departure is allowed, where the bond is choice, not chain. Captivity thrives on guilt. Freedom thrives on consent. Build relationships where walking away is possible, and paradoxically, you'll find fewer reasons to want to.

Designing anti-traps doesn't mean you'll never stumble into a snare again. You will. But when you do, the architecture you've built — optionality, values, constraints, reversibility, voluntary community — will make the bars thinner, the exits closer, the price cheaper. The goal isn't immunity. It's resilience. To design for escape before you even need it.

Anti-traps aren't theories. They're habits in motion, guardrails that keep your life from ossifying into cages. If you want proof, look at the people who seem strangely immune to collapse. When the market dips, they pivot. When a job ends, they rebound. When a relationship fractures, they mourn but keep moving. From the outside, it looks like luck. From the inside, it is designed. They've built lives that bend instead of break.

Take money. Captivity loves debt. Debt narrows options, chains the future, forces obedience. Anti-traps in money don't mean hoarding wealth; they mean shaping financial life so you can exit at will. A man I knew made less than many of his peers but was freer than all of them. Why? He kept expenses low, avoided consumer debt, and saved not for retirement but for maneuverability. "I don't need much," he said. "That's my shield." He couldn't be bullied by employers or banks because his freedom didn't require a giant salary. He had designed money as a tool, not a leash.

Look at work. Most careers are cages dressed as ladders. The higher you climb, the narrower the rungs. Anti-traps mean designing a career as a portfolio, not a path. I knew a woman who refused promotions past a certain point because she realized management would tie her to politics instead of her craft. Instead, she built side projects, diversified her skills, and treated her employer as one client among many. Colleagues thought she lacked ambition. What she lacked was captivity. She retired early, not because she won the game, but because she refused to play it.

Relationships tell the same story. Love can be a bond or a cage, depending on whether exit is allowed. Anti-traps in relationships don't mean casual connections with no loyalty. They mean loyalty that renews voluntarily. The strongest marriages I've seen are not the ones where leaving is unthinkable, but where leaving is possible and therefore staying is a daily choice. One couple I knew celebrated their anniversary by asking each other, "Do you still choose this?" It wasn't a threat. It was a ritual of freedom. Because the door was unlocked, they both knew they stayed not from fear but from desire.

Even belief systems can be designed as anti-traps. Tradition, ideology, religion — these can nourish, but they can also imprison. The difference is whether doubt is allowed. An anti-trap faith permits questions, even departures, without branding them betrayal. An anti-trap ideology permits revision when reality shifts. Captivity begins the moment doubt is silenced. Freedom begins when doubt is part of the structure. I once knew a pastor who told his congregation, "If leaving this church is the right move for you, go with blessing." That sentence was an anti-trap in itself. It broke the bars before they could form.

Another key: anti-trap design with friction. Captivity is sticky. It thrives on convenience, inertia, and sunk costs. Anti-traps introduce deliberate friction so that staying stuck is harder than leaving. Automatic transfers into savings accounts. Calendar reminders every six months to audit commitments. A rule that every subscription renews manually, never automatically. These frictions seem small, but they make escape easier. They tilt the balance toward freedom by making captivity the harder option.

The most overlooked anti-trap is in the community. Most people design belonging as permanence: one tribe, one identity, one set of rituals forever. That design is brittle. The moment the group corrupts, you are trapped. Anti-trap community is plural, overlapping, and portable. You belong to several circles, none of which owns you entirely. If one collapses, you still stand. If one demands silence, you can speak elsewhere. A man I knew joined multiple networks deliberately, never pouring all his loyalty into one. "It's not disloyal," he said. "It's insurance." Captivity loves monopolies. Freedom loves redundancy.

This design ethic doesn't eliminate risk. Anti-traps don't make you invincible. They make you resilient. They don't stop storms. They give you multiple shelters. And resilience is the only kind of safety freedom allows. If you wait for perfect protection, you'll never leave the cage. Anti-traps accept the inevitability of risk but refuse the inevitability of capture.

People often resist designing anti-traps because it feels paranoid. Isn't it enough to escape once? Isn't constant vigilance exhausting? But vigilance isn't exhaustion when it is built into design. Think of it like engineering. Bridges don't fall because engineers assume wind and weight will test them, so they design for flex. Anti-traps are the flex of life. They prevent collapse not by resisting force but by absorbing it. If you embed that flex into your systems, you don't have to worry daily. The structure itself resists capture.

The secret is that designing anti-traps is not about building walls around yourself. It's about leaving doors open. It's about structuring life so you can always walk away from what no longer serves you. That isn't paranoia. That is the only form of loyalty that means anything. To commit while free is truer than to commit while trapped. And only anti-traps make that loyalty possible.

The resistance to designing anti-traps often comes from pride. People tell themselves they are too smart to be trapped again. They think that because they escaped once, they are immune. But freedom is not a vaccine. Escaping a cage doesn't prevent the next one from forming. In fact, escapees are often more vulnerable because they crave stability. After the chaos of leaving, the temptation of a new certainty is overwhelming. They run straight into the arms of a job, a partner, a system that promises security, and before they know it, the bars are back.

Anti-traps demand humility. You accept that you are always vulnerable. You accept that your psychology is wired to trade freedom for comfort, clarity for certainty, independence for approval. If you don't design against those instincts, they will design against you. Pride says: I'm different. Humility says: I'm human. And humans build cages without realizing it.

This is why rituals matter. Anti-traps are not one-time choices. They are habits that reinforce freedom. A quarterly review of your commitments. A monthly audit of your expenses. A yearly question to yourself: "What cage am I walking into?" These rituals are simple, but they keep you awake. Cages form in sleep. Anti-traps are built in consciousness.

I knew a man who asked himself one question every New Year: "What am I willing to walk away from this year?" Sometimes the answer was a habit, a client, or a belief. He said the point wasn't always to act, but to remind himself that everything was negotiable. That question was his anti-trap. It kept the bars from hardening unnoticed.

Fear is another barrier. People resist designing anti-traps because it feels like planning to fail. They don't want to imagine quitting a job, leaving a partner, burning a map. They want to believe this time it will last. This time it will be safe. But denial is the architect of captivity. Refusing to plan for exits doesn't keep cages away. It makes them harder to escape when they arrive. Designing anti-traps isn't pessimism. It's realism. You aren't planning to fail. You're planning to stay alive when the system does.

Another psychological trap is guilt. People believe that designing an exit is disloyal. That having savings means you don't trust your partner. That keeping skills sharp means you don't respect your employer. That staying part of multiple communities means you aren't committed to one. But the opposite is true. Anti-traps make loyalty stronger because it is chosen, not coerced. If you can leave at any time and still stay, your presence has weight. If you cannot leave and stay anyway, your presence is meaningless. Anti-traps make love real, work honest, and community alive.

One of the strongest anti-traps I've seen was built by a couple who kept separate bank accounts even after decades of marriage. People mocked them for it, accused them of mistrust. But when I asked why, the wife said, "Because I don't want either of us to feel trapped by money. I want us to stay because we want to, not because we can't afford not to." That clarity kept them freer, and paradoxically closer, than most couples I knew.

Anti-traps also force you to confront sunk costs. People cling to cages because of what they've already paid — time, money, reputation. Designing anti-traps means refusing to worship sunk costs. You remind yourself: past investment is not a reason to stay, it is a reason to reconsider. If you wouldn't enter the arrangement fresh today, you shouldn't remain because of yesterday. Anti-traps keep the door visible by refusing to nail it shut with guilt over wasted years.

It takes courage to live this way because society rewards permanence. Employers want lifetime loyalty. Communities want unquestioned commitment. Families want traditions frozen in time. To build anti-traps is to defy those rewards. You look restless. You look unstable. You look disloyal. But what you are is awake. And if you can endure the misinterpretation, you build a life that cannot be quietly stolen from you.

The most radical anti-trap is learning to love impermanence. To see endings not as failures but as completions. The job was good until it wasn't. The friendship nourished until it starved. The belief held until it cracked. Anti-traps mean blessing the ending instead of resenting it. They mean recognizing that every structure has a lifespan. Refusing to acknowledge that is what turns shelter into prison. Accepting it is what keeps you moving free.

The final element of anti-trap design is imagination. Most cages feed because we cannot imagine life beyond them. We assume debt is inevitable, burnout is natural, and dishonesty is required. We build lives around these assumptions, never questioning whether another way exists. Anti-traps begin in imagination: the audacity to picture a life where the bars are thinner, the exits closer, the air lighter. Without imagination, escape is reactive. With it, escape becomes preventive.

I once met a woman who reimagined her entire profession. She was a nurse who loved medicine but hated the bureaucracy that crushed her spirit. Rather than quit outright or surrender to the system, she created a cooperative clinic with peers. They pooled resources, stripped away excess paperwork, and designed policies together. Patients paid less, nurses were freer, and care was better. She hadn't escaped medicine; she had redesigned it. Her anti-trap was born from imagination, from refusing to accept the structure as given.

The same holds in art, in business, in relationships. The trap says: This is the way things are. The anti-trap asks: what if they weren't? That question is the hinge of freedom. It doesn't guarantee an answer, but it opens a door. Every new model, every rebellion that sticks, begins with someone willing to imagine that captivity was optional.

Anti-traps are contagious in this way. When you build them, others see that design is possible. Your refusal to sign long contracts makes your peers question theirs. Your insistence on multiple communities shows others they don't have to pledge allegiance to only one. Your transparent values make others examine the ones they swallowed whole. Anti-traps don't just free you. They loosen cages around you.

But designing anti-traps is also lonely work, because you are often the first to step away. You will be misunderstood. You will be accused of being paranoid, cynical, and uncommitted. You will be told that redundancy is cowardice, that constraints are weakness, that reversibility is indecision. The mapped world cannot fathom a design ethic built on exits. But the mapped world has never known what it is to walk free without fear of capture.

There is a discipline here that is easy to forget once you've tasted freedom: you have to maintain what you've built. Anti-traps are not self-sustaining. They erode under neglect. Optionality collapses if you stop cultivating skills. Reversibility dies if you sign commitments in a moment of exhaustion. Values blur if you don't repeat them until they become reflexive. To stay free, you must keep building. Not constantly, not obsessively, but rhythmically — like tending a garden.

I once asked a man who seemed unusually free how he did it. His answer was simple: "I prune." Every season, he cut back obligations, expenses, and even friendships that had grown too heavy. He said the pruning hurt, but it left space for growth. "If I don't prune," he told me, "the branches turn into bars." That was anti-trap design in practice: maintenance, vigilance, and pruning as survival.

The reward of this work is subtle but profound. When you live inside anti-traps, life feels lighter. You walk with less fear because you know exits exist. You love more honestly because departure is allowed. You work more fully because exploitation is harder. You breathe deeper because the bars are further apart. The wilderness is still dangerous, but you have built shelters that bend with the storm instead of crumbling under it.

The ultimate anti-trap is recognizing that freedom is never finished. There is no final escape, no moment when the work ends. There is only design and redesign, exit and re-exit, building and rebuilding. This is not failure. It is the nature of freedom itself: alive, shifting, demanding. People long for permanence, but permanence is captivity in disguise. Anti-traps embrace impermanence as the only true safety.

And so the task is not to dream of a cage-free life but to design one where cages cannot last. To shape money, work, relationships, community, belief, and time so that each resists capture. To prune, to question, to imagine, to build. It is work, yes. But it is lighter than the work of captivity. The cage demands endless endurance. Anti-traps demand creativity, vigilance, and courage. The first drains. The second sustains.

To design anti-traps is to accept that freedom will always charge a price. But it is also to decide that you will never again pay with your entire life. That is the true architecture of escape: not a single jailbreak, but a house of doors that never lock.

Anti-traps give you the structure to resist capture, but structure alone isn't enough. You can build walls that bend, doors that don't lock, and still stumble straight into a snare if you don't notice it forming. The next discipline of freedom isn't design — it's vision. The skill is learning to see the trap before you've walked into it.

Chapter 12: Learning to See

The hardest thing about traps is not breaking them. It's recognizing them early enough to avoid them. Most cages don't appear overnight. They grow slowly, strand by strand, until one day you realize the door is shut. You call it bad luck, or you blame someone else, but the truth is simpler: you didn't see it coming. You were busy, distracted, reassured by routine. By the time you noticed, the bars were already welded.

Learning to see is the discipline that keeps you from replaying the same escape over and over. Without it, you become a serial prisoner, breaking out of one cage only to stumble into another. With it, you spot the outlines before they harden. You recognize the pattern while it's still faint pencil lines, not steel rods. And that recognition is priceless. Because the cheapest trap is the one you never enter.

The problem is that humans are wired to miss the warning signs. We confuse comfort with safety. We confuse familiarity with truth. We confuse approval with belonging. Each confusion blinds us to the slow tightening. You tell yourself the long hours are temporary. You tell yourself the constant anxiety is normal. You tell yourself that silence is peace. You edit the evidence until the cage looks like home. Seeing through that fog requires training.

The first training is pattern recognition. Traps differ in surface detail, but their architecture repeats. Debt. Dependency. Silence. Loyalty demanded without reciprocity. Rules that only move in one direction. Benefits that evaporate the moment you stop conforming. Once you've seen one, you begin to see them everywhere. The employer who insists you're family but discards people like furniture. The partner who showers you with love until you disagree. The institution that praises you while extracting your soul. Different costumes, same cage.

I knew a man who described his life as "running into the same wall with different wallpaper." Job after job, relationship after relationship, the surface details shifted, but the outcome didn't. He thought he was cursed. He was blind. Once he began looking for the repeating structures—power without accountability, loyalty without freedom—he saw them clearly. The wall wasn't new each time. It was the same design in a different paint.

The second training is listening to your body. Long before your mind admits you're in a trap, your body knows. The tightness in your chest before walking into the office. The exhaustion after every conversation with a certain friend. The knot in your stomach at the thought of another holiday with family. These signals are data. They are your body's way of saying: this is not freedom. But we learn to mute them. We drown them in caffeine, distract them with screens, dismiss them as weakness. Learning to see means unmuting. Paying attention. Trusting discomfort as a warning system.

The third training is skepticism of certainty. Cages are sold with certainty. "This is the right path." "This is the only way." "This is forever." Freedom requires suspicion whenever certainty is sold too cheaply. People who promise permanence are usually selling control. People who demand forever are usually hiding fragility. When you hear certainty, ask questions. Who benefits if I believe this? Who profits if I obey? What happens if I walk away? If the answers terrify the seller, you've found a bar.

But seeing is not paranoia. It is awareness. Paranoia sees traps everywhere and collapses into paralysis. Awareness sees traps where they actually form and moves accordingly. The difference is testability. Paranoia assumes without evidence. Awareness tests, probes, gather data. Say no once and see if the world collapses. Leave one demand unmet and observe the fallout. Most traps reveal themselves when tested. If nothing happens, you weren't in one. If punishment comes swiftly, you were. Either way, you've learned.

This kind of vision is lonely at first, because you notice what others refuse to. You see the cage forming while your peers are still celebrating. You raise questions that earn you side-eyes. You become the "negative one," the "cynic," the "troublemaker." But what you're really doing is refusing to sleep through captivity. People don't thank you for this. They resent you for it. Until the bars close. Then they wish they had seen, too.

The discipline of seeing is not glamorous. It doesn't come with applause. It often looks like an overreaction, like fussing about details others ignore. But it is the difference between a life spent constantly breaking out and a life spent walking free. Escape is dramatic. Vision is quiet. But vision is what keeps escape from becoming a cycle.

Seeing is a skill, and like any skill, it can be trained. The tragedy is that we aren't taught to use it. Schools train us to follow instructions. Jobs train us to hit targets. Families train us to keep the peace. None of these rewards notices the bars. They reward pretending the bars don't exist. So when you begin to train your sight, you feel awkward, guilty, even rebellious. That's the point. You are unlearning blindness.

The first tool of training is language. Cages hide in euphemisms. "Family culture" at work means exploitation dressed as care. "Tradition" in the family often means silence around abuse. "Loyalty" in friendship sometimes means obedience to someone else's insecurities. If you accept euphemisms at face value, you won't see the trap forming. Start interrogating words. When someone says "We're like a family here," ask yourself: what does this family demand, and what does it cost to leave? When someone says, "This is just how it's done," translate it: Who benefits if it stays this way? Language exposes architecture if you stop taking it literally.

The second tool is time. Most traps rely on urgency. "Sign now." "Don't think too long." "Decide before the opportunity disappears." Urgency is the camouflage of cages. It blinds you to terms, hides the exit, and makes refusal feel impossible. The discipline of slowing down is an anti-trap in itself. Delay the signature. Sleep on the offer. If freedom is real, it will survive twenty-four hours. If it's a cage, the pressure to decide immediately is proof.

The third tool is contrast. When you're deep inside a structure, you normalize its weight. You think exhaustion is normal because everyone else is exhausted. You think silence is normal because no one else speaks. Contrast shows you otherwise. Spend time in different environments. Notice how your body feels in them. The friend group where you laugh until your ribs ache reveals the toxicity of the one where you tiptoe. The workplace where ideas flow exposes the suffocation of the one where they die. Without contrast, traps feel inevitable. In contrast, they glow.

Another tool is small disobedience. Traps depend on compliance. Test them with resistance. Say no to a meeting. Skip a ritual. Speak a forbidden truth. If the punishment is disproportionate, you've exposed a bar. If nothing happens, you've exposed the illusion of one. Either way, you learn. This is why systems loathe small disobedience: it reveals the weakness of their architecture. You don't have to stage a rebellion to see the cage. You only have to scratch the paint.

But seeing isn't only about others. The most insidious traps are the ones you build yourself. You trap yourself with perfectionism, with the need to be liked, with stories you tell about what you can or cannot do. To see these, you need a mirror. Journals, therapy, conversations with brutally honest friends. The goal isn't comfort. The goal is exposure. Ask yourself: what am I unwilling to question? Whatever the answer, that's where the bar is hiding.

There is a temptation to believe that once you've trained your vision, the work is done. But traps evolve. They adapt to your awareness. You leave one job because it demanded obedience, then stumble into another that flatters your ego instead. You end one relationship because it silenced you, then enter another that drowns you in noise. Seeing is not a one-time achievement. It is an ongoing discipline, like sharpening a blade. Let it dull, and you'll miss the next snare.

The irony is that once you can see, you can never return to blindness. You will notice cages everywhere: in advertising, in politics, in families, in friends. At first, this feels exhausting. You wonder if the whole world is a prison. But in time, the vision becomes empowering. You realize the bars were always there; you simply see them now. And seeing them doesn't doom you. It frees you. You don't stumble in by accident. You choose. You test. You walk with eyes open. That alone is power.

The discipline of seeing doesn't stop at the personal. Once your sight sharpens, you begin to notice how entire systems are designed as cages. You watch an industry praise innovation while quietly ensuring no one leaves the treadmill. You see how politics offers the illusion of choice while narrowing outcomes to the same corridors. You see how families pass down guilt as inheritance, ensuring obedience from generation to generation. The cages are everywhere, but so are the seams. Once you learn to see them, you realize captivity was never inevitable. It was always constructed, and what is constructed can be dismantled.

This systemic sight is unsettling because it makes you aware of how deep the patterns run. You can no longer shrug off manipulation as a coincidence. You recognize strategy in what once looked like chaos. The endless cycle of debt and consumption is not an accident—it is a design. The culture of overwork is not a quirk—it is a method of control. The silence around abuse is not ignorance—it is a traditional weaponized. Seeing this strips away innocence. You lose the comfort of believing the world is neutral. But you gain the clarity of knowing where the pressure points are.

I knew a teacher who said learning to see ruined television for her. She couldn't watch an advertisement without noticing the hooks: scarcity, status, shame. At first, she hated it—she missed the ease of being entertained. But eventually she came to love the awareness. "I feel like I'm walking through a carnival with the lights on," she told me. "The illusions don't work on me anymore." That's what vision does. It doesn't kill joy. It kills hypnosis.

Seeing also changes how you relate to people. You start noticing who is trying to trap you, and who is trying to keep you free. Some people thrive on others' captivity. They want you dependent, silent, predictable. Others thrive on your freedom. They celebrate your choices even when they differ from theirs. When you see the difference, your relationships shift. You stop wasting energy on those who need you chained. You pour into those who want you unbound. This filtration is painful—you lose connections you once called central. But what remains is cleaner, sharper, truer.

Another unsettling effect of seeing is that you become harder to manipulate. Compliments lose their sting if you notice the demand beneath them. Threats lose their bite if you recognize the bluff. Promises lose their shine if you see the trap door hidden in them. This doesn't make life easy, but it makes it clear. You begin to move differently, less reactive, more deliberate. And people notice. Some respect it. Others resent it. Either way, you are no longer easily caught.

But sight is not enough unless you act. Many people stop at awareness, congratulating themselves for seeing cages everywhere. But recognition without action becomes its own trap. You grow cynical, detached, paralyzed. You see everything as manipulation and retreat from the world entirely. That's not freedom. That's another form of captivity, a cage made of suspicion. The discipline is to pair vision with movement. To see clearly, and then to choose clearly.

Seeing traps in culture also tempts you to believe you must dismantle them all. But that's impossible. The point is not to save the entire world. The point is to refuse to be unconscious in it. You may never topple an industry or transform a culture. But you can walk through it awake. You can refuse its bars, even if others accept them. And that refusal is contagious. The moment you live awake, others notice. They begin to question. They begin to see.

The paradox of vision is that it isolates and connects at the same time. You feel alone when you first see what others miss. But you also find your tribe: the ones who are awake too. They might be rare, but they exist. And when you meet them, you recognize each other instantly. The conversations are different. The energy is different. You don't have to explain why cages are suffocating. They already know. Seeing is not just a personal discipline. It is the doorway to a community of the awake.

The final discipline of seeing is not detection. It is integration. Spotting traps is only the beginning; learning to live with eyes open is the real challenge. Many people glimpse the bars once or twice, panic, and then retreat into blindness again. They convince themselves it was imagination, or they bury the discomfort in routine. But vision is like a muscle. If you don't use it, it atrophies. If you keep exercising it, it sharpens until it becomes second nature.

Integration means building life rhythms that keep your sight clear. Journaling is one. Not the kind filled with achievements, but the kind that records dissonance: the days you felt smaller, the conversations that drained you, the moments you said yes when you meant no. Those pages, revisited, expose patterns you'd miss in the rush. Another rhythm is conversation. Find people who won't let you sleepwalk. The friend who notices when your tone dulls, the partner who asks why your energy has shifted, the mentor who names the compromises you don't want to admit. Seeing together is stronger than seeing alone.

Integration also means learning to trust intuition without worshipping it. Intuition is often dismissed as irrational, but in truth, it is data your body has already processed faster than your conscious mind. The dread in your stomach before a meeting, the joy that lights your chest after a conversation, the sense of suffocation in a house that looks perfect on paper—these are signals. But they are only signals. Test them. Probe them. Respect them without idolizing them. Intuition plus verification is vision. Intuition alone can become paranoia.

The more you integrate seeing into life, the more you discover that clarity itself is a form of wealth. Most people are poor in clarity. They spend their lives in cages that profit from confusion, handing away their agency because they never learned to question what was handed to them. Clarity doesn't guarantee happiness. It doesn't make pain disappear. But it gives you the ability to choose pain instead of having it chosen for you. That difference is the heart of freedom.

The danger of vision is that it never ends. Once you can see, you cannot stop. You'll notice the trap in the advertisement, the snare in the contract, the hidden bar in a friendship. At first, this feels heavy, like the world is one endless prison. But with time, it becomes lighter. Because you realize that the bars were always there, you simply see them now. And seeing them doesn't condemn you. It equips you. Awareness is not a burden; it is armor.

I knew a man who said once he learned to see, he felt like he had ruined his life. He couldn't tolerate the job he had, the marriage he was in, or the friendships he kept. Everything looked like a cage. He thought vision had cursed him. But years later, after rebuilding, he said something different: "It wasn't that vision ruined my life. It ruined my illusions. And illusions were all that was holding me." That is the true power of seeing. It doesn't destroy your life. It destroys your ability to lie to yourself. And that is the most dangerous freedom of all.

The last lesson of vision is gratitude. Not because traps vanish, but because once you see them, you can step around them. You can choose differently. You can refuse to inherit cages passed down by families, corporations, or cultures. You can walk lighter. You can help others open their eyes, not with lectures but with presence. You live awake, and in doing so, you permit others to do the same. That ripple is not dramatic, but it is real. Seeing spreads.

Learning to see is not glamorous. It will not make you popular. It will not earn applause. But it will keep you free. It will keep you from sleepwalking into the same prisons everyone else calls normal. And it will sharpen your sense of life itself, because when the bars are visible, so is everything else. Color is brighter. Breath is deeper. Connection is cleaner. When you live awake, you don't just avoid traps. You experience freedom as a daily reality, not a rare event.

This is the shift: escape is no longer a crisis you wait for. It is a posture you live in. Vision turns freedom from a rare jailbreak into an ongoing habit. And that habit is what makes everything that follows possible. Because once you can see, you can choose. And once you can choose, you are no longer captive.

Sight sharpens your freedom, but vision alone doesn't keep you safe. The danger of seeing too much is mistaking clarity for endless possibility. Once the bars are visible, you want to tear them all down, to seize every open door. But freedom without limits can harden into a new kind of trap. The paradox is simple: too much freedom becomes captivity in disguise.

Chapter 13: The Freedom Paradox

The irony of freedom is that it can trap you as effectively as captivity ever did. Once you've broken out, once the bars have bent and the map has burned, the rush is intoxicating. No more obligations, no more scripts, no more ceilings. The air feels infinite. And yet, that infinity can choke you. Too much choice is another prison, only this one is invisible. You wake up every day staring into an open horizon, and instead of liberation, you feel paralysis. The paradox of freedom is that without shape, it collapses into chaos.

People rarely admit this because it sounds ungrateful. After all, they fought to get free, they paid the bill in blood and doubt, they earned their escape. To then confess that freedom itself feels suffocating seems like betrayal. But the feeling is real. Without boundaries, without purpose, freedom becomes weightless, and weightlessness is terrifying. You drift. You spin. You wonder if maybe the cage wasn't so bad after all, because at least there you had a direction.

This is why some escapees crawl back. They mistake structure for captivity, and when freedom offers them none, they miss the false solidity of their old walls. They confuse uncertainty with meaninglessness. They confuse openness with emptiness. And so they run back to the first job, the first relationship, the first belief system that offers them a script. They mistake surrender for relief. The paradox swallows them whole.

But the problem isn't freedom itself. The problem is unshaped freedom. Pure possibility with no anchors is as unlivable as pure captivity. A life designed without limits becomes a void. You end up chasing stimulation, novelty, indulgence—not because you want them, but because they're there. Hedonism is just another kind of trap: endless pleasure that leaves you numb. Nihilism is another: endless openness that leaves you inert. The paradox is that to stay free, you must choose constraints. Voluntary, conscious, deliberate constraints.

I once knew a man who left corporate life with enough savings to never work again. At first, he celebrated: travel, leisure, freedom without end. But within two years, he was broken. His days blurred into nothing. He drank too much, drifted too far, and nearly destroyed himself. Then he set a rule: he would create something every day, even if no one else saw it. That constraint saved him. It gave his freedom shape. It reminded him that liberation is not the absence of structure. It is the ability to choose the right structures.

The paradox is sharpest in relationships. People escape controlling families or suffocating marriages and swear off commitment entirely. For a while, it feels like freedom—no obligations, no compromises. But eventually, the openness becomes loneliness. They realize that connection requires limits. Love demands commitments, and commitments, if chosen freely, are not cages. They are chosen walls that keep the house warm. The paradox is that you cannot live free by avoiding all boundaries. You live free by building the ones that matter.

The same applies to work. Some people leave rigid careers and vow never to be tied down again. They freelance, gig, and drift from project to project. At first, it is exhilarating. But without some anchor—without a throughline of meaning—they lose momentum. Their freedom erodes into exhaustion. What saves them is not another cage, but a chosen focus: one craft, one mission, one purpose that channels the energy instead of dispersing it.

The paradox is that freedom must be shaped, or it devours itself. And shaping requires the very thing you once escaped: structure. The difference is who designs it. Cages are built for you. Structures are built by you. One is control. The other is a choice. The work of living free is not endless avoidance. It is a disciplined construction.

The paradox of freedom shows up most brutally when possibility collides with psychology. Human beings crave agency, but they also crave clarity. When every option is open, the mind short-circuits. Psychologists call it "decision fatigue," but in practice, it feels like despair. You stand in front of the open horizon, every door wide, and instead of walking through one, you collapse. This is the failure point of unshaped freedom: possibility without direction becomes paralysis.

I once spoke with a woman who had escaped a suffocating corporate career. She dreamed for years of being free to pursue her art, and when she finally walked away, she celebrated like a prisoner at dawn. For months, she reveled in her days: no meetings, no boss, no deadlines. But soon the freedom turned on her. Every day, she faced an ocean of hours and a thousand choices. Paint or write? Stay or travel? Rest or push? Each option felt loaded, each path heavy. She began to dread the mornings. "I thought freedom would feel light," she told me, "but it feels like drowning." What saved her wasn't more freedom. It was rules she made for herself: mornings were for painting, afternoons for reading, evenings for friends. Structure saved her from collapse.

This is the lesson many refuse to accept: the opposite of captivity is not chaos. The opposite of captivity is design. Freedom erodes into chaos without a chosen form, and chaos collapses into despair. People who escape cages and then reject all structure often find themselves in the arms of nihilism. They feel unmoored, adrift, unable to find meaning. In that emptiness, new cages look seductive. At least a cage gives direction. That's why so many who swear never to return end up back inside. They mistake the relief of structure for the necessity of captivity.

The freedom paradox explains why revolutions so often fail. Nations overthrow tyrants, burn down the old system, seize the intoxicating openness of possibility. But within months or years, they collapse into new dictatorships. Why? Because freedom without shape leaves a vacuum, and vacuums pull in strongmen. If people don't design new structures, the old patterns reappear in disguise. The same dynamic plays out in personal life. Burn the map, destroy the cage, walk into the wilderness—if you don't shape your freedom, the first manipulator who offers you certainty will own you again.

There's another layer to the paradox: freedom can enslave you through indulgence. Many mistake liberation for license. They drink too much, sleep too much, and spend too much. They gorge on options until their bodies, minds, and spirits collapse. The hedonist thinks he is free because he answers to no one. But he has simply built a new cage: one ruled by appetite. Pleasure without discipline hardens into compulsion. And compulsion is captivity by another name.

I knew a man who inherited wealth young. With no need to work, he celebrated his independence. He traveled, partied, and indulged. He was free—or so he thought. Within a decade, he was hollow, addicted, broken. His freedom had rotted into slavery to his own appetites. "I thought I escaped the system," he said, "but I became my own warden." The paradox crushed him. What he lacked wasn't freedom. It was the discipline to shape it.

This is where constraints return, not as cages but as lifelines. Freedom thrives inside limits chosen consciously. The runner who sets a distance, the artist who chooses a medium, the entrepreneur who fixes a principle: these constraints don't imprison, they empower. They channel possibility into purpose. Without them, freedom disperses into nothing. With them, freedom becomes force.

The paradox also reveals itself in community. People leave controlling families or institutions and vow never to be bound again. They float from group to group, terrified of belonging. At first, this feels like independence. But soon it curdles into loneliness. Humans need connection. The anti-trap isn't avoiding community—it's choosing communities where loyalty is voluntary. Freedom means saying yes to connection without surrendering the right to say no. Those who refuse to belong at all discover that isolation is just another prison.

The real paradox is that true freedom is built on self-chosen boundaries. You can only stay free by limiting yourself. This offends people who dream of escape as endless openness. But endless openness is a mirage. Without limits, freedom becomes self-destruction. With limits, it becomes sustainable. The runner collapses without a finish line. The musician meanders without a key. The liberated collapse without structure. Limits don't betray freedom. They keep it alive.

There's a phrase that captures this paradox perfectly: "Freedom is not the absence of rules, but the presence of the right ones." Cages are rules imposed on you. Structures are rules you choose for yourself. The difference is authorship. Captivity is submission to someone else's design. Freedom is submission to your own. The paradox is that without submission to anything, you dissolve. To remain free, you must bind yourself—but only to principles you choose, to constraints you can revise, to purposes you believe in.

This is not a compromise. This is survival. The addict is free to indulge every appetite, but dies enslaved. The drifter is free to avoid every tie but dies alone. The rebel is free to destroy every rule, but dies meaninglessly. Only the one who shapes freedom with self-chosen limits survives awake. The paradox isn't a flaw in freedom. It is its architecture.

The paradox of freedom is not only personal. It is cultural. Societies that achieve high levels of individual liberty often stumble into the same trap: abundance of choice collapses into paralysis or decadence. Look at civilizations at their peaks— Rome drowning in excess, Weimar Berlin spiraling into chaos, empires unraveling not because of invasion but because freedom metastasized into indulgence. Too much liberty without discipline hollowed them out from within. The same story plays out in modern lives. When everything is possible, nothing feels necessary. The abundance that was supposed to liberate ends up suffocating.

I once taught a group of young entrepreneurs in a program designed to foster innovation. They had resources, networks, and almost no restrictions. They could build anything they wanted. What happened? Most of them built nothing. The sheer openness paralyzed them. One confessed, "I miss when I had a boss telling me what to do. At least then I knew where to start." This is the paradox in miniature: liberation without shape becomes overwhelming. Freedom requires scaffolding, or else it collapses under its own weight.

You see the same in consumer culture. Walk into a supermarket with five options and you choose happily. Walk into one with five hundred and you freeze, resent the decision, and wonder if you chose wrong. The science is clear: more options often lead to less satisfaction. This is why modern societies filled with abundance are also filled with anxiety and depression. We thought endless choice would give us joy. Instead, it gave us exhaustion. Captivity suffocates, but endless possibility drowns.

The paradox is sharper in personal identity. People once lived with rigid roles: farmer, merchant, priest, soldier. The cages were real, but so was the clarity. Now roles are fluid, identities are open, choices are endless. At first, this feels liberating—until it doesn't. People now drown in the pressure to "be anything." With no boundaries, the self dissolves. This is why so many cling to identities handed to them by movements, brands, or communities.

They aren't lazy. They are overwhelmed. They want shape. Without it, freedom feels like formless chaos.

I knew a man who quit his job to travel the world. He posted photos from beaches, mountains, cities, living the dream of absolute freedom. But after a year, he was depressed. "I thought I'd feel alive," he told me, "but every day just feels empty." He had escaped structure but failed to replace it with meaning. He had confused escape with purpose. The paradox consumed him: the very freedom he worshipped became the source of his despair.

The paradox also explains why cults, authoritarian leaders, and manipulative institutions thrive even in free societies. People escape one control system, but when they meet the void of possibility, they panic. The first voice that offers certainty, the first leader that promises clarity, the first group that offers belonging becomes irresistible. Freedom without discipline makes people easy prey. They surrender their agency willingly, not because they love captivity, but because they can't tolerate the void.

That void is what anti-traps are meant to prevent. Structures of your own making. Rules you choose. Communities you select. But even anti-traps require vigilance. If you forget why you built them, they calcify into cages again. The budget that once gave you optionality becomes dogma. The principle that once gave you focus becomes rigidity. Even self-chosen boundaries can become prisons if you stop revising them. The paradox doesn't vanish with good design. It demands constant re-engagement.

Another danger of the paradox is the illusion of infinite time. When you first break free, you imagine you have forever. No boss, no deadlines, no obligations. You'll write the book later. You'll launch the project later. You'll deepen the relationship later. Later becomes never. Freedom without urgency is another kind of death. The cage forced urgency upon you. Now you must manufacture it yourself. Without urgency, freedom becomes procrastination.

I once met a writer who inherited wealth and retired young. He dreamed of producing novels now that he was free from work. But decades later, he hadn't written a word. "Every day I thought I had time," he told me. "Now I realize time was the only thing I didn't have." Freedom tricked him with the illusion of infinite tomorrows. The paradox wasn't that he lacked liberty—it was that liberty without urgency killed his drive.

This is where purpose enters. Purpose is not a cage if chosen freely. It is a compass. The paradox teaches that freedom must be pointed toward something larger than itself. If freedom is only freedom from, it collapses. It must also be freedom for. For building. For creating. For loving. For living. Without that orientation, freedom decays into decadence or despair.

The paradox is also intergenerational. Parents who escape cages often overcorrect. They give their children limitless freedom: no rules, no guidance, no constraints. They think this is love. But children without boundaries grow anxious, lost, and insecure. They need rails to feel safe. Not cages. Rails. The same paradox applies at scale: too little freedom crushes. Too much freedom dissolves. Balance is survival.

The cultural myths of freedom make the paradox worse. We glamorize the rebel with no ties, the wanderer with no plan, the billionaire who answers to no one. We call this freedom. But the truth is, most of these figures are miserable. The wanderer becomes lonely. The billionaire becomes paranoid. The rebel becomes irrelevant. The myths seduce us into thinking freedom is infinite openness, when in fact freedom is sustainable only when shaped.

Here is the uncomfortable truth: freedom requires responsibility. Not the responsibility imposed by others, but the responsibility you take on yourself. The responsibility to shape time, to choose values, to set boundaries, to design structures. This is not a weakness. It is a strength. The paradox is that freedom demands more discipline than captivity ever did. Captivity outsourced responsibility. Freedom hands it back. Many cannot bear the weight.

And yet, this is what makes freedom real. To accept the paradox is to stop running from boundaries and start designing them. To accept that the only way to remain free is to shape your life deliberately, to bind yourself to what matters, to prune constantly, to resist the drift of chaos. The paradox doesn't make freedom impossible. It makes freedom meaningful.

The final lesson of the freedom paradox is that it cannot be solved, only managed. People waste years searching for the perfect balance: enough freedom to feel alive, enough structure to feel safe. They dream of a final design, a system that guarantees both forever. But life won't allow it. The balance shifts with age, with circumstance, with the seasons of your own soul. What frees you at twenty may trap you at forty. What sustains you in crisis may suffocate you in peace. The paradox isn't an equation to crack. It's a rhythm to learn.

Rhythm means checking in often. Asking yourself not just "Am I free?" but "Am I drifting?" Too many constraints and you slide toward captivity. Too much openness and you dissolve into chaos. The art of freedom is walking that line, revising as you go. This is not failure. This is maturity. Freedom is not a state you arrive at. It is a practice you maintain.

I once knew a man who lived in rigid cages for decades before finally breaking free. When I asked how he kept himself from collapsing into chaos afterward, he shrugged. "I review my life like a pilot checks instruments," he said. "Am I too rigid? Too loose? Too heavy? Too light? If I don't adjust, I crash." That image stuck with me. Freedom is flight. It requires constant correction. Ignore the instruments, and the sky swallows you.

The paradox also demands honesty about cost. To stay free, you will sacrifice things that others prize. Stability. Predictability. Applause. You will be misunderstood, even pitied. People will call your chosen constraints weakness, your self-designed structures eccentric. They will not understand that the rules you've built are not prisons but protections. You can't expect them to. Most have never lived outside cages long enough to know the difference. The paradox is lonely because few people are willing to bear its tension.

And yet, those who do discover something profound: freedom is not lightness alone. It has weight. Not the crushing burden of captivity, but the grounding weight of self-authorship.

It is the difference between carrying your own pack across open ground and dragging someone else's chains. Both are heavy. One is chosen. One is not. The paradox teaches you to carry willingly, not resentfully. To embrace the weight of freedom as proof that you are alive.

The final danger of the paradox is despair—the temptation to decide that if freedom requires structure, then maybe cages aren't so bad after all. But here is the truth: chosen structure may feel similar on the surface, but its essence is different. Captivity dictates. Freedom designs. Captivity punishes dissent. Freedom revises. Captivity demands permanence. Freedom allows endings. The difference is subtle but absolute. To surrender that difference is to betray yourself.

What remains, then, is a simple mandate: build boundaries that serve you, tear them down when they no longer do, repeat endlessly. Accept that freedom is not endless openness, but endless authorship. Accept that the paradox never disappears, but can be harnessed. Accept that you will never escape the need for shape, only the danger of shape imposed by others.

The reward of this acceptance is peace. Not the shallow peace of certainty, but the deeper peace of knowing you are awake. You will still stumble, still drift, still overcorrect. But you will not live blind. You will not confuse chaos for freedom or cages for safety. You will walk the paradox with eyes open. And that is enough.

Because in the end, freedom is not measured by how wide the horizon looks. It is measured by whether you can walk toward it without chains. The paradox doesn't weaken that truth. It sharpens it. You remain free not by refusing all structure, but by refusing to surrender authorship. That refusal is the essence of escape.

Living inside the paradox teaches you that freedom isn't a single act but a discipline. You break out, you design, you see, you revise. But even with vision and structure, life pulls you back toward cages. The only way to resist capture long-term is to live by principles—rules not imposed from outside but carried within. This is where escape stops being an event and becomes a code.

Chapter 14: The Escape Artist's Code

The difference between someone who escapes once and someone who stays free for life is a code. Most people stumble out of cages by accident or by desperation. They recognize a trap too late, they pay the price in pain, and they claw their way into the open. But without a guiding set of principles, they drift right back in. Freedom without a code is temporary. A code turns escape into a habit instead of an anomaly.

Codes have existed for as long as people have sought freedom. The Warriors had codes. Monks had codes. Sailors and explorers lived by codes. These weren't arbitrary rules; they were distilled survival strategies, ways to carry clarity into hostile terrain. The escape artist is no different. Once you live outside the cage, the world sees you as dangerous, unstable, a threat. You need principles to hold you steady—not bars, but anchors.

The first rule of the escape artist's code is minimal commitments. Cages feed on overload. Every yes you give, every contract you sign, every promise you make without thinking becomes a bar. The escape artist learns to say no reflexively. Commitments are entered only with clarity and only when they serve freedom rather than suffocate it. This doesn't mean avoiding responsibility. It means choosing responsibility like a scalpel, not a net. You don't drown in obligations because you never let them pile that high.

The second rule is optionality above optimization. The world worships efficiency—squeeze every drop, maximize every hour, refine every process. But optimization narrows paths until only one works. The escape artist designs life for flexibility instead. A job that allows skills to travel. Money set aside not for more consumption but for more exits. Relationships that thrive on choice instead of coercion. Optionality means never letting yourself become hostage to a single point of failure.

The third rule is clarity of values. Without clear values, you are easy prey. Institutions, partners, and leaders all manipulate fuzziness. They tell you that loyalty is love, that sacrifice is virtue, that silence is peace. If you haven't carved your values into bedrock, you will obey theirs. The escape artist repeats their values like a mantra: what I will trade, what I will not. What I will cut, what I will carry. With clarity, traps lose their bait.

The fourth rule is the willingness to walk away. This is the escape artist's sword. Captivity thrives on your fear of leaving— fear of losing money, status, approval. The code flips that fear into strength. You remind yourself daily: I can leave. The job, the house, the circle, even the identity. Nothing owns me but what I choose. Walking away isn't failure; it is freedom in action. The cage is strongest against those who can't imagine leaving. It is weakest against those who leave their default.

The fifth rule is live with lightness. Not in the sense of irresponsibility, but in the sense of not letting possessions, reputations, or labels grow too heavy to carry. Cages rely on weight: mortgages too big to move, reputations too fragile to risk, identities too rigid to shift. The escape artist keeps life portable. They cultivate skills, not titles. Relationships, not reputations. Principles, not brands. If forced to move, they can move. If forced to change, they can change. Weight kills freedom. Lightness preserves it.

I once knew a man who embodied this code without naming it. He owned little, committed to few, and walked away often. People called him unreliable. Yet he lived freer than anyone I knew. He wasn't careless; he was coded. His principles made him resilient. He was never rich, but he was never owned. He lost things often, but he never lost himself. His life looked strange to outsiders, but it was coherent. He didn't stumble from trap to trap because he carried a compass inside him.

The escape artist's code doesn't eliminate suffering. It doesn't guarantee success. It doesn't make life easy. What it does is make captivity harder. It builds into you the reflexes of refusal, the instincts of resilience, the discipline of design. With a code, you don't have to invent an escape every time. You simply follow the rules you've already chosen.

The code sharpens in practice, not theory. Principles are only as strong as the moments they're tested. Anyone can talk about minimal commitments until someone they love demands a promise that feels suffocating. Anyone can preach optionality until the high-paying job offers security in exchange for silence. The code is not philosophy. It is behavior under pressure. That's where freedom either collapses or hardens.

Take minimal commitments. The world will always call you selfish for refusing to overload. Employers want more hours, families want more sacrifice, and friends want more loyalty. The escape artist's answer isn't coldness. It's clarity. You can say no with warmth. You can refuse without cruelty. The code demands discipline, not because you want to hoard your energy but because you know the cost of overcommitment. Every unnecessary yes is a link in the chain. The world won't understand this. They will call you cold, detached, unreliable. But they are not the ones who will pay your bill in regret. You are. The code demands you guard your yes with your life.

Optionality comes under attack in subtler ways. Companies offer you golden handcuffs: pensions that mature only if you stay, promotions that tether you to politics, perks that look like gifts but are really glue. Friends and partners do the same: conditional love, loyalty that collapses if you shift, approval tied to obedience. The escape artist resists not because they dislike stability but because they see its danger. True stability isn't dependency—it's redundancy. You don't put all your weight on one rope. You weave many. That's optionality in motion.

Clarity of values is the most dangerous part of the code, because once you state your values, you are accountable to them. Many avoid clarity because it's easier to bend when things get hard. But the escape artist engraves values into bone. If integrity is non-negotiable, then you leave the job that demands dishonesty, even if the salary is dazzling. If health is non-negotiable, then you end the relationship that corrodes your body with stress. If curiosity is non-negotiable, then you walk away from the circle that punishes questions. Values hurt in practice. That's why they matter.

The willingness to walk away is the code's most feared principle. It terrifies others because it cannot be controlled. The moment people know you can leave, they lose leverage over you.

This makes you dangerous to employers, partners, and even systems. It also makes you lonely. Many cannot handle the idea that love, loyalty, or community could coexist with the door unlocked. But the escape artist knows the opposite is true: locked doors kill love. Freedom to leave keeps relationships alive. This principle doesn't mean fleeing at the first sign of difficulty. It means refusing to stay once captivity begins. The difference is everything.

Living with lightness sounds simple, but it may be the hardest discipline of all. The world trains you to accumulate—possessions, titles, identities. You think each one makes you safer. But weight is a cage disguised as comfort. The more you carry, the harder it is to move. The escape artist trains in subtraction: fewer possessions, fewer masks, fewer anchors. This doesn't mean asceticism. It means designing life so nothing owns you. A house you can sell without collapsing. A career you can pivot without humiliation. A reputation you can shed without losing your sense of self. Lightness isn't poverty. It's mobility.

These principles sound stark, but they don't lead to isolation. They lead to a sharper connection. When you refuse to overcommit, your yes matters. When you build optionality, you show up by choice, not coercion. When you live your values, people know who you are. When you are willing to walk away, every stay is authentic. When you live lightly, your presence isn't buried under baggage. The code doesn't hollow out relationships. It strengthens them.

The most important part of the code is remembering that it isn't fixed. A rigid code becomes another cage. Principles must be revisited, revised, and refined. What served you in one season may imprison you in another. The code is alive. It breathes with you. This is why journaling, reflection, and review matter. The escape artist isn't free because they follow rules blindly. They are free because they question even their own code.

I once knew a woman who built her life around the code but forgot this last piece. Her values were clear, her commitments minimal, her lightness remarkable. But she froze the code in place. She refused to evolve it as her life shifted. The principles that freed her at thirty were suffocating her at fifty. When she finally revised them, she said it felt like escaping twice. The lesson is sharp: even self-chosen rules can become prisons if you refuse to rewrite them.

The code is not about perfection. It is about reflex. It is about carrying principles so deep in your bones that when the moment of pressure comes, your instincts act before your fear does. To live coded is to train until refusal is natural, until walking away is muscle memory, until lightness feels like home. The code doesn't make you invincible. But it makes captivity improbable.

The code is not meant to be hidden. It isn't a secret creed you whisper to yourself in the dark. It becomes real only when you live it publicly, in full view of those who will misunderstand it most. And they will misunderstand. The world is built to reward captivity. Those who live by the code threaten the arrangement. Employers call you disloyal. Families call you selfish. Friends call you unreliable. But in truth, you are dangerous not because you betray them, but because you reveal to them how easily they betray themselves. The code is not rebellion for its own sake. It is survival.

This survival begins with the way you treat time. Captivity eats your hours and then your years. It fills calendars with obligations you didn't choose. The escape artist's code treats time as sacred, non-renewable, the foundation of every choice. Minimal commitments mean refusing to let others colonize your time. Optionality means building your calendar with exits in mind. Clarity of values means your hours match your principles, not someone else's. Lightness means you can shift when life shifts. Walking away means you won't stay chained to a schedule that starves you. Time is the raw currency of freedom. To code your life without protecting it is to miss the point.

The code also governs how you deal with a crisis. Captivity seduces with the illusion of safety: pensions, marriages, reputations that promise stability. But when a crisis comes, those bars don't hold; they collapse on you. The escape artist's code flips the logic: resilience over stability. Optionality means you can pivot jobs when one collapses. Lightness means you can relocate when disaster hits. Minimal commitments mean you aren't buried under obligations when you need to move fast. Willingness to walk away means you never confuse collapse with the end of life. Clarity of values means you can lose nearly everything and still know who you are. That is survival.

But survival isn't enough. The code also has to nourish. Captivity kills slowly by stripping meaning. You're busy but hollow, comfortable but numb. The code refuses that trade. Optionality gives you space to pursue curiosity. Clarity of values aligns your daily acts with what matters. Minimal commitments preserve energy for what's alive. Walking away keeps you from the slow death of resignation. Lightness makes room for joy. The code doesn't just keep you alive. It keeps you awake.

I once knew a man who seemed reckless to everyone around him. He quit jobs others would have killed for. He ended relationships that others envied. He sold his house with barely a second thought. But when I asked why, he smiled: "Because I'd rather be wrong than trapped." His code wasn't about perfect choices. It was about keeping the exits visible. He wasn't reckless. He was coded. And because of that, he had fewer regrets than anyone I knew.

The code reshapes the community, too. Traps often form through belonging: families, workplaces, movements that demand obedience in exchange for connection. The escape artist's code builds community differently. You surround yourself with people who respect exits. Friends who don't guilt you when you decline. Partners who celebrate choice rather than demand sacrifice. Colleagues who understand loyalty as voluntary. These communities are rare, but once you find them, they feel like oxygen. They prove that freedom and connection are not enemies. They can coexist, but only if the code is shared.

This is why the code spreads. People notice when you live differently. They may resent it, but they also admire it. You become the friend others confide in when they're suffocating. You become the colleague others ask about when they're burning out. You become the quiet reminder that another way exists. The code is contagious because captivity is miserable. Even those who resent your freedom can't ignore its pull.

The code also hardens your relationship with failure. Captivity teaches you to fear failure above all. That's why cages dangle stability—because failure seems lethal. But the escape artist knows failure is survivable. Failure is just another exit, another map to burn, another principle to refine. The code ensures that when you fail, you don't collapse. You pivot. You re-route. You try again. Failure inside captivity is humiliating. Failure outside is education.

Living by the code also forces you to wrestle with reputation. Captivity thrives on external validation. Do what's expected, and you'll be praised. Resist, and you'll be shamed. The code requires letting the reputation die. To live coded is to accept being misunderstood, mischaracterized, even slandered. You must know yourself so clearly that applause and condemnation weigh the same. That kind of resilience terrifies people, but it's also magnetic. Those who crave freedom will find you. Those who crave captivity will despise you. Either way, you are no longer controlled.

The paradox of the code is that it doesn't guarantee peace. It guarantees conflict. Every principle in it collides with the world. Minimal commitments clash with others' demands. Optionality clashes with institutions that thrive on dependency. Clarity of values clashes with cultures built on compromise. Walking away clashes with loyalty myths. Lightness clashes with consumerism. To live by the code is to live at odds with the dominant order. But conflict is not defeat. It is proof that you are awake.

What the code gives in exchange is coherence. Your life may look chaotic from the outside—job shifts, geographic moves, relationships ended—but inside, it is consistent. You know why you stayed. You know why you left. You know what you trade and what you refuse. Captivity offers stability without coherence. The code offers coherence even in chaos. That difference is freedom.

The last rule of the escape artist's code is the one that threads all the others together: remember you are temporary. Every cage, every escape, every structure you build will pass. Freedom is not eternal; it's renewed daily. The code exists to remind you that vigilance is not paranoia—it is life.

Temporary means you do not cling. To possessions. To identities. To communities. To victories. You carry them lightly, knowing they can serve you now and betray you later. You refuse to mistake the tool for the truth. A job is a tool. A partner is a choice. A community is a shelter. None of them is destiny. Forget this, and even the brightest freedom will harden into a cage.

The code also demands generosity. Freedom that exists only for yourself curdles into selfishness, and selfishness is another prison. The escape artist understands that sharing the code strengthens it. When you live by example, when you help others see their exits, you expand the field of freedom. This doesn't mean rescuing anyone—you can't. But you can stand as proof that another way exists. You can be the one who leaves and thrives, so others can believe it's possible. The code multiplies in this way, not through preaching, but through presence.

To live by the code is to accept loneliness. Not always, not forever, but often. Most of the world is not ready to walk away from its cages. They'll look at your principles and see arrogance, instability, and immaturity. They'll tell themselves stories to explain away your freedom, because to admit the truth would threaten their own choices. The escape artist's code doesn't protect you from misunderstanding. It prepares you for it. It steels you against the hunger for approval. You are not coded to be loved. You are coded to remain free.

Yet paradoxically, the code also opens you to deeper love. Because when you live coded, every yes is real. Every bond is chosen. Every stay is authentic. You cannot be blackmailed into affection, bribed into loyalty, or guilted into connection. Those who walk beside you know it is because you want them there, not because you have no choice. This is love sharpened by freedom, rarer and stronger than the cheap imitation captivity calls devotion.

The code is not romantic. It doesn't make life easy or simple. What it does is anchor you in clarity so that you do not drift back into cages. It gives you rules sharper than convenience, stronger than temptation, deeper than fear. With it, you can face crisis, temptation, and manipulation, and still stand. Without it, you are always one compromise away from capture.

The final truth of the code is that it must remain alive. Static rules become cages. Living rules remain weapons. You revise them, question them, and refine them as your life shifts. You prune commitments, expand optionality, reaffirm values, test your willingness to walk away, and practice lightness. You do this not once, but constantly. The code breathes with you. That is what keeps it from becoming another prison.

What the escape artist's code gives you is not invulnerability. It gives you resilience. It gives you the ability to survive collapse, betrayal, failure, and remain yourself. It gives you coherence when the world demands conformity. It gives you a compass when the map burns, a rhythm when chaos swirls, a spine when pressure mounts. The code is not optional. It is the price of staying free.

The day you abandon the code is the day you drift back into captivity. You won't notice at first. The bars will look familiar, comfortable, even loving. But you will feel the tightening eventually. And if you have forgotten the code, you will not have the reflexes to leave. That is the danger. Freedom without a code is a temporary holiday. Freedom with a code is a life.

To live by the code is to live strange, misunderstood, light, and alive. It is to carry principles that others mock but secretly envy. It is to walk away when others cannot. It is to stay awake while others sleep. And it is to keep the exits visible, always, no matter how beautiful the room looks. The code doesn't promise happiness. It promises clarity. And clarity, in a world built on cages, is freedom itself.

The code keeps you free, but freedom itself is not the end of the story. Escaping, designing, seeing, and living by principles— all of it matters only if it leads somewhere worth going. Otherwise, escape is just an endless cycle of jailbreaks. The real test is what life looks like once the bars are gone, once you've built a rhythm that keeps you free. This is life on life beyond the bars.

Chapter 15: Life Beyond the Bars

Life after escape is quieter than people imagine. The movies teach us to expect fireworks, parades, and triumphant music as the gates swing open. In truth, freedom feels less like victory and more like stillness. There is no roar of applause. There is silence, and inside that silence, the strange weight of your own choices. For the first time, no one is telling you what to do. You have to decide. That silence is terrifying at first. Then it becomes holy.

On life beyond the bars, you learn that freedom doesn't erase scars. It reveals them. You carry the wounds of captivity into the open, and at first, they ache worse than before. When you were trapped, you could blame the cage for everything. Out here, you see how much of the damage is yours to heal. Escape doesn't erase fear or shame or regret. It forces you to face them without excuses. This is why some people romanticize the cage after leaving. They forget the suffocation and remember only the simplicity. But the truth is, the scars don't mean you failed. They mean you survived. And survival is the foundation of a different kind of life.

The first difference you notice on the outside is time. In captivity, time was stolen. The hours belonged to bosses, institutions, and expectations. Days blurred together, and years disappeared without your permission. In life beyond the bars, time stretches. At first, it feels almost unbearable—so much space, so much responsibility. But slowly, you realize that this is what life is supposed to feel like. Afternoons aren't obligations.

Evenings aren't countdowns. Time is yours, and with it, the possibility to shape meaning.

The second difference is breath. Captivity compresses you. You breathe shallowly, your body curled around stress, your chest tight with unspoken fear. Outside, your breath deepens. It doesn't happen all at once, but one day you notice yourself inhaling without flinching, exhaling without dread. That breath is not just oxygen. It's a declaration: I am not owned. You begin to breathe into possibilities you never allowed yourself before—art, love, movement, silence. You discover that breath itself can be joy when it isn't rationed by survival.

The third difference is attention. Captivity narrows your gaze. You watch the bars, the routines, the rules. Your vision collapses to the immediate. On life beyond the bars, your sight expands. You notice the sky again. You notice the way people laugh, the way ideas spark, the way the world hums when you aren't drowning in duty. Freedom trains you to look outward instead of inward, forward instead of down. That shift in attention is subtle but radical. It's the difference between endurance and living.

I once spoke to a woman who had left an abusive marriage after decades. She told me the hardest part wasn't leaving. It was realizing, a year later, that she could laugh without asking permission. "I didn't even know I was allowed to enjoy things," she said. "Freedom isn't just leaving the cage. It's remembering you can live outside it." That is the essence of life beyond the bars: rediscovering permissions you never should have needed in the first place.

Life on life beyond the bars is not easy. Bills still exist. Fear still lingers. Loss still hurts. Freedom is not the absence of difficulty. It is the presence of choice. You can choose which bills to pay with which work. You can choose which fears to confront and which to let dissolve. You can choose which losses are worth the grief. Captivity steals that agency. Freedom restores it. The circumstances don't vanish, but the weight shifts. Life feels heavy when it is forced upon you. It feels lighter when you carry it yourself.

The greatest revelation on life beyond the bars is that freedom sharpens life's edges. Captivity dulls everything. The food, the days, the conversations all blur. Outside, everything feels sharper: the sweetness of friendship, the sting of betrayal, the depth of silence. People sometimes say freedom is overrated because it doesn't erase suffering. But they miss the point. Freedom doesn't erase suffering. It makes joy and suffering both more vivid. You live the highs higher and the lows more honestly. That intensity is what makes life worth living.

And then there is love. Love on life beyond the bars feels different because it is voluntary. In captivity, love was entangled with obedience. You stayed because you had to. You silenced yourself because you feared losing approval. Outside, love becomes sharper, riskier, but real. When you say yes, it matters. When someone stays, it matters. The fragility of it makes it stronger. You realize that the only love worth keeping is the kind that survives freedom. Anything else is just captivity in disguise.

On life beyond the bars, you learn a new paradox: freedom is not the end of the story. It is the beginning of another. You thought escape was the climax. It is only the prologue. The work now is not to keep escaping forever but to build, to live, to expand. Freedom is not a finish line. It is a foundation.

The longer you live outside, the more you realize that freedom is not defined by absence but by presence. At first, the thrill comes from what is gone—the boss, the cage, the constant surveillance. But soon the question shifts: what fills the space now? Freedom is empty unless it is inhabited. Life beyond the bars isn't just about breaking patterns. It's about writing new ones.

The first arena where this shows is work. In captivity, work was extraction—your hours traded for someone else's gain. On life beyond the bars, work becomes expression. It doesn't mean every task is bliss, but it means your labor is no longer hollow. You do things. They connect to values. They sustain the life you actually want, because they sharpen you instead of deadening you. Sometimes this means entrepreneurship, sometimes art, sometimes simply finding employment that aligns with your rhythm instead of draining it. The difference is not whether the labor is hard, but whether it belongs to you.

I knew a man who left a corporate career and began repairing bicycles for a living. On paper, it looked like regression. His salary shrank. His title vanished. But his life expanded. "I work harder now than I did in the office," he told me, "but none of it feels like theft." The work wasn't easier. It was his. That was the difference of life beyond the bars: the dignity of authorship.

The second arena is relationships. Outside the cage, connections lose their scripts. You stop measuring them by longevity or obligation and begin measuring them by vitality. You no longer stay because you must. You stay because it matters. This makes relationships fewer but deeper. The friends who survive are the ones who thrive in the oxygen of choice. The partners who survive are the ones who can handle the unlocked door. It is terrifying to live this way because people can leave. But it is also liberating, because when they stay, it is real.

One couple I knew renewed their vows every five years with no guarantees in between. They called it "choosing again." People thought it was reckless, but it was the opposite. It was coded love: tested, voluntary, alive. Their bond didn't weaken because of the unlocked door. It strengthened because of it. Life on life beyond the bars made their marriage sharper, more honest, and far more resilient than the ones built on fear.

The third arena is identity. Captivity defines you by the cage: your title, your role, your obedience. Outside, identity is fluid. You can change careers, cities, even names without collapse. At first, this feels disorienting—if you are not what the cage called you, who are you? But in time, it becomes exhilarating. You are not a label. You are a process. You are what you choose and re-choose, not what someone stamped on your forehead. Life beyond the bars dismantles the illusion of permanence. It teaches you that identity is alive.

This fluidity is frightening for people who crave certainty. They ask you to define yourself, to stabilize, to freeze. You frustrate them because you won't. But that frustration is freedom's proof. You are no longer legible in the way captivity

179

demands. You are illegible, and illegibility is survival. It means you cannot be caged as easily.

The fourth arena is community. Outside, belonging is no longer monopolized. You don't give your whole self to one tribe or ideology. You diversify your bonds, creating resilience in connection. If one group collapses or corrupts, you don't collapse with it. You remain standing because you were never owned. This plural belonging is misunderstood. People accuse you of disloyalty. But loyalty without freedom is not loyalty. It is coercion. Life on life beyond the bars redefines community not as permanence but as consent.

The fifth arena is self-trust. Captivity trains you to distrust yourself. Rules and scripts tell you what to think, how to behave, and when to act. Outside, you have no script but your own. At first, this is paralyzing. What if you choose wrong? What if you fail? But with each decision, each experiment, each recovery from failure, you learn that self-trust is built, not given. Freedom sharpens your faith in yourself because it forces you to test it constantly. Life beyond the bars doesn't eliminate mistakes. It integrates them into strength.

All of these arenas—work, relationships, identity, community, self-trust—show the same truth: freedom is not a single act of leaving. It is the ongoing act of inhabiting. Life beyond the bars is not utopia. It is raw, vivid, demanding. It asks you to stay awake when sleep would be easier. It asks you to choose when drifting would be simpler. It asks you to carry the weight of authorship instead of letting someone else carry it for you.

The reward is coherence. Your days match your values. Your work matches your rhythm. Your relationships match your choice. Your identity matches your evolution. Your community matches your consent. Your self-trust matches your scars. Coherence doesn't mean ease. It means wholeness. And wholeness is the one thing captivity can never give.

Life on life beyond the bars doesn't just change you. It changes how you see the world around you. Once you've breathed outside the cage, you can't look at society the same way. What once seemed normal now looks absurd. The endless commutes, the pointless meetings, the loyalty to institutions that never reciprocate — all of it looks like theater performed inside a prison yard. You begin to notice how many people confuse comfort with freedom. They talk about choices while never exercising them. They praise stability while living in quiet panic. Life beyond the bars gives you vision, and that vision is double-edged. It gives clarity, but it also isolates.

This is why people who have escaped often struggle to re-enter old circles. They find themselves biting their tongue at dinners, unable to play along with conversations about promotions, mortgages, or reputations. It isn't arrogance; it's dissonance. They've seen what life can feel like without chains, and it's hard to pretend the chains don't rattle. Some learn to stay quiet, nodding politely while inside they feel the gulf widening. Others withdraw, unwilling to pretend. Life beyond the bars shifts not just your choices but your capacity for pretense.

I knew a man who left the military after twenty years of service. He stepped into civilian life and found himself bewildered by how people lived. "Everyone acts free," he told me, "but they move like they're following orders." He struggled to connect because he couldn't unsee the invisible cages. Eventually, he built a new circle of people who had also escaped something — prison, cults, corporations, toxic families. "It's like we recognize each other," he said. "We've all seen the bars." That is one of the defining traits of life beyond the bars: a new kind of kinship, not built on shared cages, but on shared exits.

Generationally, life beyond the bars looks different, too. Younger people who grow up in relative abundance sometimes mistake endless options for freedom, only to discover that their lives are filled with invisible cages — debt, digital addiction, the pressure to brand themselves constantly. Older people who spent decades in captivity often step out with deeper gratitude, but also deeper grief. They mourn the years stolen, the versions of themselves that never got to exist. Both perspectives carry truth. The young battle the paradox of too much freedom. The old wrestle with the ache of lost time. Life beyond the bars sharpens these differences. It doesn't erase them.

Culturally, life outside the cage can feel like heresy. Whole systems rely on people believing that captivity is normal. Economies depend on debt, employers depend on dependency, religions depend on obedience, and families depend on silence. When you live outside, you puncture these illusions simply by existing. Your refusal to participate exposes the trap. That exposure threatens those still inside. They'll call you reckless, selfish, even dangerous. In a way, they're right. Life beyond the bars destabilizes captivity by showing that it is not inevitable. Freedom is a contagion.

The psychology of life beyond the bars is equally complex. At first, freedom feels intoxicating — the rush of new choices, the relief of open air. But then comes the aftershock: guilt. Survivors often feel they've betrayed those who remain inside. They wonder if leaving makes them selfish, if staying would have been nobler. Some even sabotage themselves, returning to captivity out of loyalty. But the truth is harsher and kinder: you cannot free others by staying trapped with them. You can only free them by walking out and showing the door exists. Guilt fades when you realize your responsibility is not to remain caged but to remain visible.

Another challenge is abundance. Outside, the question is no longer "How do I endure?" but "What do I do with possibility?" That shift is liberating but also destabilizing. Possibility can feel like pressure. You have all this freedom, so shouldn't you be extraordinary? Shouldn't you achieve more, build more, love more? This is another trap: the captivity of perfection disguised as potential. Life beyond the bars teaches you to resist this, too. Freedom is not an obligation to greatness. It is permission to live honestly. Sometimes that means achievement. Sometimes it means rest. The point is not to maximize freedom. The point is to inhabit it.

Life beyond the bars also sharpens your relationship with risk. Captivity dulls risk because decisions are made for you. Outside, you face risk daily — financial, emotional, social. At first, this is terrifying. Then it becomes normal. You learn to fall, to fail, to recover. Risk stops being an enemy and becomes a teacher. You realize the worst outcome isn't failure. It's captivity. That realization makes you bolder. You try more, experiment more, because the cost of failure is lighter than the cost of bars.

Over time, life beyond the bars redefines success. In captivity, success is obedience rewarded: the promotion, the approval, the applause. Outside, success is coherence: living in alignment with your values, regardless of applause. I once asked a woman who had left a high-status career if she missed the recognition. She laughed. "I miss being impressive," she said, "but I don't miss being hollow." That is the difference. The cage gave her status. Life beyond the bars gave her soul.

Living free also changes how you see endings. In captivity, endings feel like disasters—losing a job, ending a relationship, walking away from tradition. On life beyond the bars, endings feel like openings. They hurt, but they also breathe. You no longer see them as collapsing. You see them as pruning. Every ending makes space for something aligned. This doesn't make endings easy. But it makes them survivable. More than that, it makes them meaningful.

Life beyond the bars isn't paradise. It's not free from fear, pain, or loss. But it is real. It is sharp. It is awake. Captivity numbs. Freedom intensifies. On life beyond the bars, you don't escape suffering—you choose it. You choose the work worth sweating for, the love worth risking for, the values worth bleeding for. That is what makes life beyond the bars more than survival. It makes its life.

The final truth of life beyond the bars is that freedom is not permanent. It is a practice, a rhythm, a discipline renewed each day. The cage doesn't vanish forever just because you left it once. The world is full of new ones waiting, dressed in opportunity, affection, or certainty. Even self-chosen structures can harden into bars if you stop tending them. Freedom lives not in escape alone, but in vigilance and design.

But here is the gift: once you've crossed to life beyond the bars, you know the way out. You've carried yourself through collapse before, and that memory is a weapon. You know that even if you stumble into a snare, you can cut your way free again. That knowledge is power. Captivity depends on convincing you there is no alternative. Life beyond the bars proves otherwise. You will never again forget the taste of air.

What people rarely understand is that freedom is not about grandeur. It is not the mountaintop, the revolution, the dramatic scene. It is the texture of daily life: mornings that belong to you, decisions made without coercion, love offered without fear. On life beyond the bars, the extraordinary is the ordinary—because ordinary life itself has been reclaimed from captivity. You discover that drinking coffee without dread is a victory, that laughing without permission is a revolution, that walking away without collapse is wealth.

Life beyond the bars also changes how you imagine the future. In captivity, the future was a script: retirement, promotions, milestones, anniversaries. Outside, the future is unwritten. That can feel terrifying, but it also means possibility. You are not condemned to repeat what came before. You can reimagine, redesign, and reinvent. Life beyond the bars gives you back authorship of time.

The most surprising part of freedom is gratitude. At first, it is anger that dominates—anger at the years lost, at the manipulation endured, at the versions of yourself that never had a chance. But as you live further outside, gratitude deepens. You realize that even the scars serve. They remind you of what you survived. They sharpen your resolve not to return. They give you empathy for others still inside. Gratitude doesn't erase the rage. It holds it alongside relief, making life richer and sharper than captivity ever could.

And finally, life beyond the bars teaches you this: freedom is not about leaving everything behind. It is about carrying forward what matters. You don't abandon love, curiosity, integrity, or creativity. You abandon fear, silence, and obedience. What you carry becomes lighter because you've chosen it. What you leave behind no longer drags you. That is the final difference between captivity and freedom: in captivity, life carries you. On life beyond the bars, you carry life.

So what is life on life beyond the bars? It is not perfect, not utopian, not free of pain. It is vivid. It is awake. It is coherent. You walk with scars, but also with clarity. You know what you will trade and what you will not. You know how to design, how to see, how to walk away, how to stay. You know that freedom is fragile and fierce at once, and that its value comes not from ease but from sharpness.

And when the cages call again—and they always do—you know the answer. You have already crossed once. You can cross again. Life on life beyond the bars is not a promise. It is a practice. But it is the only practice that makes life worth living.

Escape begins with panic, sharpens into discipline, and settles into practice. You design, you see, you code, and finally you inhabit. Life on life beyond the bars is not the end of the story but the opening of one. And yet, books must close even when lives don't. An epilogue belongs here—not to wrap freedom in neat bows, but to remind you that escape is not an achievement, it is a posture.

What follows isn't a conclusion. It is an invitation.

Epilogue

The Practice of Escape

When you look back, escape never feels like a single act. At the time, it might have looked dramatic—the resignation letter, the packed suitcase, the final slammed door. But in memory, it dissolves into a thousand smaller movements: the questions you started to ask, the unease you stopped silencing, the doubts you finally allowed to breathe. Escape, when told honestly, is less about breaking chains than about noticing you were shackled in the first place.

That is why the epilogue matters. Not because it ties a bow around everything, but because it names what was always true: escape is unfinished. It is a practice, a posture, a discipline. You do not graduate from it. You live inside it. Some days it sharpens you like a blade. Other days, it feels like a burden you'd trade for the numbness of captivity. Freedom is fragile. It is fickle. It is exhausting. And yet, it is the only thing that gives life any edge at all.

On life beyond the bars, the temptation is to mythologize escape as a story of heroes. But there are no heroes here. There are only ordinary people learning to walk away from what harms them. Ordinary people realize that cages are not destiny. Ordinary people carrying scars into daylight. If you romanticize it too much, you'll miss the grit, the exhaustion, the loneliness. Escape costs. It tears holes in your relationships, your finances, and your sense of identity. To live free is to carry wounds. But those wounds are cleaner than the rot captivity breeds.

One truth that reveals itself after enough time outside is that escape is not evenly distributed. Some people are born closer to exits. Others are locked deeper inside by systems, histories, or legacies heavier than any single individual can bear. To talk about escape without acknowledging this is dishonest. Privilege opens doors. Oppression welds them shut. But even in the deepest captivity, there are cracks, seams, moments of choice. The practice of escape does not mean everyone walks out into the same field. It means everyone learns to push where the bars are weakest, to keep vision alive even when the exits are distant.

What, then, does it mean to live as an escape artist? Not to burn everything constantly, not to live rootless, but to hold life with a kind of flexible grip. To accept that endings will come and to let them. To prune without apology. To revise without shame. To design without worshipping permanence. To love without chaining. To belong without surrendering. The escape artist is not free because they never stumble into cages. They are free because they never stay in them once they see.

Freedom, at its deepest, is less about breaking away from others than about breaking away from your own illusions. The illusion that you can't live without that job. The illusion that your family's approval is oxygen. The illusion that comfort is safety. The illusion that you need permission. Escape burns these illusions until you are left with something starker: yourself, unadorned, uncoerced, unshielded. That nakedness is terrifying, but it is also the raw material of real life.

I once asked a man who had rebuilt his life after losing everything what freedom meant to him. He didn't talk about money or travel, or even safety. He said, "It means I can tell the truth and survive the consequences." That sentence captures what the entire journey leads to. Freedom is not perfection. It is the ability to live honestly without collapsing. To speak, to act, to love, to walk—all with the knowledge that you can bear what follows. That is what life on life beyond the bars sharpens you for.

The practice of escape does not end when the book closes. It does not wait for crises. It threads through the mundane: how you spend a Tuesday, how you answer an email, how you sit with silence. You are always designing, always revising, always choosing. Sometimes you drift and wake up in bars you thought you'd left forever. Sometimes you build anti-traps so strong you forget the cage was ever possible. The point is not perfection. The point is practice.

And practice has a rhythm. See, design, test, walk, repeat. The cycle never ends. The difference is that, with time, it becomes lighter. Less like an emergency and more like instinct. Less like rebellion and more like breathing. You stop needing to prove it to anyone, even yourself. You simply live. And that, perhaps, is the quietest but sharpest form of escape: when freedom no longer feels like spectacle, but like the only way to move through the world without suffocating.

If there is one danger in life beyond the bars, it is forgetting. Forgetting how suffocating the cage was. Forgetting how easily the bars disguised themselves as love or duty. Forgetting how much you once believed you couldn't survive without them. Memory is not nostalgia here—it is armor. Every scar you carry is a reminder of the bars you broke. The moment you forget, you drift back, seduced by promises of safety. Captivity loves amnesia. Freedom requires remembering.

This remembering is not just personal. It is generational. Every culture carries stories of escape—slaves who fled plantations, dissidents who resisted regimes, migrants who crossed oceans. Those stories are not just history. They are survival maps. They teach that captivity, however normal it feels, is never natural. They prove that resistance is possible, even when the odds are grotesquely unfair. When we forget those stories, we weaken. When we keep them alive, we sharpen the edge of our own escape.

The practice of escape is also communal. Too often, we imagine freedom as solitary—the lone rebel walking away, the individual who breaks chains. But no one escapes alone. Even when the act looks solitary, it rests on the shoulders of others who taught, inspired, protected, or paved the way. On life beyond the bars, you begin to see this web. You realize your own exits were widened by others, and your exits, if you live well, can widen life for those who follow. Escape is contagious. Your refusal gives others courage. Your survival proves the possibility. The code multiplies because someone has to see it embodied before they believe it is real.

This is why life beyond the bars carries responsibility. Not to save others—you can't—but to remain visible. To prove that life outside exists. Some will resent you for it. Others will reach for you because of it. You do not have to carry them. You only have to remain a signal, a living contradiction to the myth that cages are destiny. This is how escape scales—not through manifestos, but through lived evidence.

The future of escape will always be fraught, because power never surrenders willingly. Every system learns from those who leave it. Employers learn how to tighten contracts. Families learn how to weaponize guilt. Institutions learn how to camouflage control more subtly. Captivity evolves. But so does freedom. The practice of escape is adaptive. Every new cage teaches a new crack to exploit, a new seam to pry open. The work never ends. But neither does the possibility.

Generationally, the practice of escape also looks different depending on the traps of the time. For some, it was war and famine. For others, it was industrial labor or domestic confinement. For us, it may be digital addiction, consumer debt, or the myth of endless productivity. The cages change costumes. The practice does not. See. Name. Walk. Repeat. The forms are new, but the discipline is old. That is why the stories matter. They are not quaint folklore. They are manuals.

One day, someone will look back at our era and marvel at the cages we accepted as normal. They will wonder how we gave so much of our attention to machines, how we traded years for jobs that despised us, how we confused scrolling for connection. They will see what we were blind to. Just as we look back at old systems and marvel that people endured them. The lesson is not that we are wiser. The lesson is that cages always feel natural when you're inside them. Only the practice of escape keeps them visible.

Life beyond the bars also raises a quieter question: what is freedom for? If escape is only about survival, then freedom risks collapsing into endless cycles of flight. But freedom that matures is freedom oriented toward creation. The free build. They compose music, start families, design communities, craft businesses, and tend gardens. They don't build cages—they build shelters, bridges, oases. Structures that hold but do not trap. That is the gift of life beyond the bars: not just leaving, but shaping. Not just survival, but art.

And this is the point most people miss. Escape isn't about abandoning everything. It's about carrying the best forward. You don't renounce love because love once caged you. You don't renounce community because community once suffocated you. You learn to rebuild both in ways that resist capture. This is why the practice never ends. Because every new structure can decay into bars. Every new bond can calcify into chains. The work is to keep them alive, flexible, breathable. To prune before the branches harden into branches. To bless endings before they rot into prisons.

So, what does the future of life beyond the bars look like? It looks like people remember more quickly when they stumble. It looks like communities are normalizing choice instead of obedience. It looks like families raising children with unlocked doors. It looks like systems are being challenged not just at their collapse points, but in their subtle routines. The future of life beyond the bars is not utopia. It is vigilance embedded into culture, resilience passed down like inheritance.

Freedom is not permanent. But neither is captivity. Both require maintenance. Both require imagination. Both rely on belief. The difference is that captivity thrives on fear, and freedom thrives on courage. Fear can silence, but courage can spread. Even one act of courage can widen a crack into an exit. That is why the practice matters. It does not promise perfection. It promises possibility.

Freedom changes not only how you live but how you think about death. Captivity tricks you into imagining that safety will protect you from mortality. If you just obey the rules, stay inside the lines, follow the script, you'll be rewarded with permanence. But the truth, which life beyond the bars forces you to confront, is that nothing spares you from the end. Death comes whether you lived caged or free. The difference is whether you spent your life rehearsing obedience or practicing escape.

People who live in cages often reach old age and realize they were never truly alive. They confuse longevity with living. They kept breathing, but they never chose, never cut, never risked. In life beyond the bars, you come to terms with mortality earlier. You stop pretending you can outwit it. You stop waiting for permission to begin. You understand that every day in freedom is already a victory, because it's one more day stolen back from systems that would have claimed you.

This awareness of mortality sharpens legacy. In captivity, legacy is usually defined by titles, inheritances, and institutions.

In freedom, legacy is carried in different currencies: stories, presence, and courage. What survives you is not what you accumulated but the exits you widened. Did your children grow up with doors unlocked? Did your friends learn from your refusal? Did your community inherit a little more air because you lived awake? These are the questions of life beyond the bars. Legacy is not monuments. Legacy is proof that you refused the bars.

I once spoke with a teacher who spent decades in a rigid school system before finally walking away. When I asked her what she wanted her students to remember, she said: "That I taught them they could leave my class without asking permission." It sounded small, even trivial. But she was right. That was her legacy: instilling in children the muscle memory of leaving when they chose, not when someone else dictated. That is what freedom looks like at scale: not grand rebellion, but small permissions multiplied.

Living long enough outside also reveals the traps you almost missed. You look back with sharper eyes and see where you nearly stayed too long, where you convinced yourself the bars were love, where you told yourself the cage was temporary. This hindsight can sting, but it also deepens compassion. You stop mocking those still inside. You remember how hard it was to see. You realize you were blind, too, until something cracked the illusion. Compassion is a life beyond the bars' quiet gift. It softens arrogance. It makes you patient. It lets you guide without preaching.

Another lesson that emerges with time is rhythm. At first, escape feels like crisis management: break, cut, burn, flee. Later, it becomes cyclical. You notice patterns of drift and correction. You notice when commitments are piling up too high, when weight is growing too heavy, when clarity is blurring. Instead of waiting until collapse, you prune earlier. You reset before the cage locks. This rhythm turns escape from drama into maintenance. And maintenance, while less glamorous, is far more sustainable.

This rhythm also applies to love. On life beyond the bars, you stop looking for permanence and start valuing renewal. You don't cling to partners, friends, or communities out of fear. You ask instead: Is this still alive? Are we still choosing each other freely? This rhythm requires courage, because it means letting go when something has died. But it also means the bonds that remain are vibrant, not stagnant. Love without cages feels riskier but tastes sharper. Every stay is authentic. Every yes is real.

The longer you live outside, the more you learn to trust impermanence. Captivity convinces you that permanence is safety. Freedom shows you that impermanence is truth. Houses sell. Jobs end. Relationships shift. Health falters. Nothing endures untouched. But instead of despair, impermanence becomes relief. You realize you don't have to carry everything forever. You only have to carry what matters now. And you can put it down when it turns into bars. This trust in impermanence keeps you light. It keeps you from mistaking stability for life.

There is also humor in life beyond the bars, though it takes time to find it. Once the panic of escape fades and the scars stop stinging, you begin to laugh at the absurdity of what once held you. You remember the meetings you thought were sacred, the approval you thought was oxygen, the debts you thought defined you. You laugh because the bars were never as strong as you believed. You laugh because you see how fragile captivity really is when tested. This humor is not cynical. It is liberating. It keeps bitterness from calcifying. It lets you carry the practice with a lighter step.

Eventually, life beyond the bars gives you a gift that captivity never could: coherence. Your days line up with your values. Your work reflects your principles. Your relationships echo your choices. You are not split between the life you endure and the life you dream of. They are the same. This doesn't mean every day is joyful or successful. It means every day is yours. That coherence is rarer than wealth, rarer than stability, rarer than applause. It is the true treasure of life beyond the bars.

And perhaps the most radical shift of all is that freedom teaches you to love differently. Not just others, but yourself. In captivity, self-love sounds indulgent, selfish, naive. In freedom, self-love is survival. You care for yourself not to escape responsibility but to remain strong enough to keep walking. You rest, not as laziness, but as rebellion against the cage's demand for endless grind. You forgive yourself, not to excuse failure, but to keep scars from becoming shackles. Love on life beyond the bars is not soft. It is fierce. It is the discipline of treating yourself as worth keeping free.

None of this makes life beyond the bars easier. If anything, it makes it sharper. But that sharpness is what makes it real.

Captivity blunts life until it is tolerable. Freedom sharpens it until it cuts. You bleed more. You laugh harder. You risk deeper. You regret it, honestly. You love fiercely. You end cleanly. That is what life on life beyond the bars demands: not numbness, but intensity. And that is why it is worth everything it costs.

The last truth of escape is that it never really ends. You don't graduate into permanent freedom. You don't cross some final line and live forever untouched by traps. You live awake, and that wakefulness keeps you moving. The bars shift, the costumes change, the illusions evolve, but the practice remains. See, design, test, walk, repeat. That rhythm is what sustains you. It is not perfection. It is vigilance.

And yet, vigilance doesn't have to be exhausting. Over time, it becomes a way of being. Just as a seasoned traveler learns to spot scams instinctively, just as a craftsman feels flaws in the grain of wood before others see them, you learn to notice cages before they close. It becomes second nature. Not paranoia, but presence. You stop living reactively and start living responsively. That is the quiet power of life beyond the bars: not just breaking free once, but carrying freedom inside your reflexes.

The final cost of freedom is loneliness. The practice sets you apart. You will always feel a little estranged from those who cling to cages, a little out of sync with the conversations built on obedience. But the final gift is kinship. Out here, scattered and rare, are others who carry the same scars. You recognize them by the way they hesitate before committing, by the way they laugh at things others take too seriously, by the way their eyes linger on exits. These people become your tribe—not because you share the same cage, but because you share the same refusal.

Together, you form communities that are fragile but real. Communities that survive not on coercion but on choice. Communities that endure because leaving is always possible. These are the only communities worth belonging to, because they do not confuse loyalty with captivity. They are shelters, not prisons. Oases, not fortresses. On life beyond the bars, you discover that freedom is not solitary after all. It is rare, but it is shared.

The practice of escape also shifts how you imagine the world itself. You stop believing in utopias—perfect societies where everyone is free forever. You know better. You know cages will always form, because power will always tempt, and fear will always seduce. But you also stop believing in inevitability. You know cages can be broken, seams can be pried, illusions can be shattered. You live between cynicism and naivety: awake, alert, unwilling to surrender, unwilling to despair. That posture is freedom's truest expression.

In the end, escape is not about being untouchable. It is about being unownable. No job owns you. No relationship owns you. No institution owns you. Even your own past doesn't own you. You remain free because you refuse to surrender authorship. You remain free because you accept endings, because you prune, because you walk when you must. Freedom is not immortality. It is self-authorship in a world that constantly tries to ghostwrite your life.

When people ask what life beyond the bars feels like, I tell them it feels like breath. Not dramatic. Not cinematic. Just breathe—deep, uncoerced, yours. It feels like mornings that belong to you. It feels like laughter you didn't rehearse. It feels like walking away without collapsing. These are not fireworks, but they are everything. They are life itself.

So the book ends here, but the practice does not. When you close these pages, you return to your own cages, your own exits, your own rhythms. The practice is yours now. You will fail sometimes. You will forget sometimes. You will drift into bars without realizing it. But you will also remember. You will also cut. You will also leave. And each time you do, you will deepen the muscle memory of freedom.

Escape is not a story you read. It is a life you live. And if there is any final invitation, it is this: live it awake. Live it sharp. Live it free enough that when the bars come—and they will—you will see them, name them, and walk out breathing.

About the Author

Jonas Calder is a writer and observer of systems—those that bind us and those we build to keep ourselves free. His work draws from a career spent inside institutions where silence was rewarded and obedience was survival, and from the long practice of learning to walk away. He writes not as a theorist but as someone who has lived through cages of his own making and others' design.

The Book on Escape is his first work under this name. It is part testimony, part guide, and part manifesto for those who feel the invisible bars and want to cut through them. Jonas lives between coastlines, keeps his possessions light, and believes that freedom is sustained not by luck but by vigilance.

About The Publisher

Welcome to The Book On Publishing

At The Book On Publishing, we believe in rewriting the rules of learning. Whether you're chasing your next big idea, building a better life, or simply curious about what should have been taught in school, you've come to the right place.

We're a platform built for dreamers, doers, and lifelong learners, offering bold, practical books and tools that empower you to take charge of your journey. From real-world skills to mindset mastery, we publish the book on what matters.

No fluff. No lectures. Just what you need to know, delivered with clarity, purpose, and a spark of curiosity.

Start exploring. Start growing. Start writing your story.

Read more at https://thebookon.ca.

Acknowledgment of AI Assistance

Portions of this book were developed with the support of AI. While every word has been carefully reviewed and refined by the author, AI served as a valuable tool for brainstorming, editing, and structuring ideas. Its assistance helped accelerate the creative process and bring clarity to complex topics.

www.ingramcontent.com/pod-product-compliance
Lightning Source LLC
Chambersburg PA
CBHW071327120626
46546CB00002B/467